SOCRATES

A(lfred) E(dward) TAYLOR was born in 1869 and was educated at Oxford. He was a member of the philosophy faculty of McGill University (1903–08) and the University of St. Andrew's (1908–24). He was appointed Professor of Moral Philosophy at the University of Edinburgh in 1924 where he remained until 1941. He died in 1945.

His works include: *The Problem of Conduct* (1901), *Elements of Metaphysics* (1903), *St. Thomas Aquinas as a Philosopher* (1924), *Plato: The Man and His Work* (1927), *Philosophical Studies* (1934), *The Christian Hope of Immortality* (1938), and *Aristotle* (1943). He has made several translations of Plato.

SOCRATES was first published in 1933 in England, and, in America, in 1952.

SOCRATES

by

A. E. TAYLOR

DOUBLEDAY ANCHOR BOOKS
Doubleday & Company, Inc., Garden City, New York

Reprinted by arrangement with
The Beacon Press, Boston, Mass.
Printed in the United States

*To the Boys and Masters of
Kingswood School, Bath*

CONTENTS

SOCRATES

I

INTRODUCTORY

The life of a great man, particularly when he belongs to a remote age, can never be a mere record of undisputed fact. Even when such facts are plentiful, the biographer's real business is with their interpretation; he must penetrate behind mere events to the purpose and character they disclose, and can only do so by an effort of constructive imagination. And in the case of both the historical figures whose influence on the life of humanity has been profoundest, Jesus and Socrates, indisputable facts are exceptionally rare; perhaps there is only one statement about each which a man might not deny without forfeiting his claim to be counted among the sane. It is certain that Jesus "suffered under Pontius Pilate," and no less certain that Socrates was put to death at Athens on a charge of impiety in the "year of Laches" (399 B.C.). Any account of either which goes beyond such a statement is inevitably a personal construction. Hence even this unpretentious sketch must be introduced by some remarks on the sources from which its writer has drawn the materials of his own construction, and the principles which have guided him in his use of them.

Socrates himself left no record of his own thought or actions. That he did not is a direct consequence of the character of the society to which he belonged. Though the part of his life of which we know most, his old age, was prolonged into a different and less happy time, Socrates was, by birth and upbringing, a man of the great age of Pericles; in fact, he was a man of over forty at the death of that statesman. Now the Athenians of those spacious days did not write books; it was an age of great tragedies, but not of prose literature. This is why, apart from one single instructive, but not absolutely certain, allusion, we have no contemporary record of anything done or said by Socrates until he was close on fifty. He was already forty-seven or more when the famous comic poets, Aristophanes and Amipsias, for some reason both selected him as the butt of their topical burlesques for the year 423 B.C.; a third comedian, Eupolis, followed suit two years later. We still possess Aristophanes' brilliant caricature, the *Clouds*, though in a version perhaps retouched by the author, and it is the only document dealing with Socrates which dates from a time before his own death.

The deep impression made by the trial and death of the philosopher led at once to the creation of a whole literature in which younger men who had come under his influence sought to preserve his memory by depicting his personality and conversation. Much of this has perished, but we still have the imposing series of dialogues in which Plato has made Socrates the central figure, the apologetic *Memorials* of the Master composed by Xenophon, with one or two minor works of the same kind from his hand, and a few pages of the Socratic dialogues of a third contemporary, Aeschines of Sphettus, and these, of course, are the main sources for any account of the philosopher. The problem is to know the right way to handle them. It is important to remember that all three writers were many years the juniors of their hero. Plato was some forty-three years younger than Socrates, Xenophon almost certainly a few years younger still, and though we have no exact dates for Aeschines, he must be roughly contemporary with the others.[1]

[1] Socrates was born in or before 469 B.C., Plato in 428/7. Xenophon in the year 401 thought himself badly

None of the three, then, can have had trust-
worthy recollections of Socrates as he was before
the age of fifty-five; when they tell us anything
of his prime, or his early life, they are not speaking from first-hand knowledge.[1]

Biography as a recognized form of literature
only appears among the Greeks in the third century B.C. (300–200 B.C.) as characteristic of the
Alexandrian age. Philosophers, like poets, had by
that time become objects of curiosity to a reading
public, and more than one writer set himself to
gratify this curiosity. The works thus produced

---

handicapped by his extreme youth when chosen one of
the generals of the retreating Ten Thousand (*Anabasis*,
III. i. 25). Hence he is not likely to have been born before about 426/25. Aeschines is mentioned by Plato
(*Apology*, 33 *e*) as a young man whose father should
have been called as a witness by the prosecutors of
Socrates if they really believed that the philosopher had
"corrupted" his son. He was the only one of the three
present at the death of Socrates (*Phaedo*, 59 *b*). Plato
(*ib.*) was lying ill, and Xenophon absent "somewhere
in Asia."

[1]Thus when Plato tells us in the *Theaetetus* of the
impression made on Socrates in the last months of his
life by the youthful hero of the dialogue (afterwards
the most eminent mathematician of the Academy), he
is writing about matters of which he had an intimate
knowledge; when he describes the meeting of Socrates
in early life with Parmenides and Zeno, he is dealing
with events which belong to a time more than twenty
years before his own birth.

have perished, but their substance is preserved for us in the *Lives of Philosophers*, which bears the otherwise unknown name of Diogenes Laertius, and, in its final form, dates from about A.D. 200. The account given of Socrates in this work remains as the chief monument of what was known or surmised about its subject by men of letters living under the Ptolemies and later. Of course it has preserved some statements of great value, substantiated by the names of the earlier authors who vouch for them. But the critical standard of the biographers of the Alexandrian age was not high. Their public demanded not so much accuracy as piquant anecdote, scandal, and repartee, and the writer had to study the taste of his public. Moreover, an author of this age was not very favourably placed for ascertaining the facts about the career of a fifth-century Athenian. The material was scanty, and consisted largely of unexplained passing allusions, often enough of topical jests in some comedy, the meaning of which was as obscure to an Alexandrian as it is to us. Biographies compiled under such conditions must not be expected to throw much light on the personality of any one, least of all on that of a man who, like Dr. Johnson, was already becoming the centre of a legend in his own lifetime. Thus for serious purposes we are thrown back almost entirely upon what we are told about Socrates by persons who could speak from their own direct knowledge, that is, in the main, upon Aristophanes, Plato, and Xenophon.

How far can we trust the representations of any or all of these writers? If certain theories widely held in the nineteenth century are sound, it would be rash to trust any of them. Aristophanes, it was said, is a comic poet, and his business is not to tell the truth but to distort it. The differences between his Socrates and those of Xenophon and Plato are so marked that we cannot take them for portraits of a single original. Either the poet and his audience must have known nothing about the ostensible hero of his play, or his object must have been something different from effective personal caricature. His satire must be pointed not at an individual but at a "movement," and we must take his Socrates, like Molière's Tartuffe, to be no more than an imaginary type, to which he has tacked the name of a particular contemporary as a label without troubling himself about the justice of the selection. Plato, no doubt, had the intimate knowledge and the dramatic gifts which might have enabled him to draw a faithful and vivid picture. But his purpose, it was generally held, was not that of the portrait-painter. His Socrates was meant either as a fancy picture of what a great philosopher should be, or as a "mask" for himself. This was supposed to be proved by alleged discrepancies between Plato's account and Xenophon's. The Socrates of Xenophon is an excellent, but rather prosy, preacher of a good, common-sense morality, with a marked dislike of unpractical speculations and "useless" science.[1] Plato's is a humorist and a great philosopher, with profound metaphysical convictions and a wide acquaintance with the highest science of his time. Hence it was assumed that the genius, the humour, the metaphysics, have been imported into the picture by Plato; they are disguised *self*-revelation.[2] It was inferred at first that the true way to get at the historical facts about Socrates is to pin our faith to Xenophon and use his statements to reduce the great figure of the Platonic dialogues to conventional proportions. (The "his-

[1] We shall see, however, that the common statements on this point ignore certain very significant passages of Xenophon himself.

[2] In particular, it was held, and is still held very generally, as a sort of self-evident postulate, that the so-called "Theory of Ideas" taught in the *Phaedo* and *Republic* must have been invented by Plato himself after the death of Socrates and before the composition of the *Phaedo*. Since the dialogue represents Socrates on the day of his death as talking of this theory as one which he has held from his early manhood, a view of this kind, if sound, would prove Plato wholly unworthy of credit in anything he tells us about Socrates.

torical Socrates," of whom nineteenth-century
writers had much to say, meant, in fact, the
Socrates of Plato with the genius taken out of
him.) On further inquiry, however, it appears
that there are good reasons for being uneasy
about the competence of Xenophon himself as a
witness. It does not appear from his own writings that he was ever particularly intimate with
Socrates, and it seems to be certain that he cannot
have been more than twenty-four at the outside
when he saw the Master for the last time.[1] In
any case, he was far away in Asia when Socrates
was tried and condemned, and his own Socratic
writings must have been composed at various in-
tervals after his subsequent return to Greece,
when he was living in exile from Athens and

---

[1] It is certain that Xenophon never saw Socrates after
his own departure from Athens in 401 to join the expe-
dition of Prince Cyrus. We do not *know* even that he
ever revisited Athens after this before his banishment
in the year 394. That he had never been very intimate
with Socrates may probably be inferred from the fact
that his name is never mentioned by Plato, who tells us
a great deal about the members of the Socratic circle.
On the other hand, Aeschines introduced into his
dialogue *Aspasia* a Xenophon who *may* be our writer,
though scholars have felt a difficulty about the identification. (The difficulty is that the Xenophon of Aeschines is a young married man, and that we have no
evidence that our Xenophon was married at so early a
date in his life.)

without much opportunity of consulting other surviving members of the Socratic circle. In some of them he tries our belief hard by attributing to the notoriously town-loving Socrates his own marked taste for farming and country life, and the most considerable of them, the *Memorabilia*, is further put out of count to an unknown extent by the fact that it has an avowedly "apologetic" purpose. It is also pointed out that there is good reason to think that Xenophon has eked out his own, probably not very extensive, recollections by using as material for his picture the very Platonic dialogues which he was at one time used to "control." This explains why there was a tendency among many of the foremost scholars at the opening of the present century to complete scepticism about the very possibility of any knowledge of the "historical Socrates."[1] An ag-

---

[1]Diels, the most eminent of them all, spoke of him as an "unknown *x*." (My immediate authority for this statement is an unpublished letter from Diels to a British scholar.) I do not reckon with the now exploded view that the incidental remarks of Aristotle about the thought of Socrates can be used as a "control" of both Xenophon and Plato. Socrates had been dead for more than thirty years when Aristotle first came to Athens, and I think it has been demonstrated by myself and others that he says nothing of any moment about the older philosopher which he might not have learned (as I have no doubt he did) from reading the Platonic dialogues. (Cf. C. Ritter, *Sokrates*, p. 83.)

nosticism of this kind must always be a melancholy *pis aller* for the historian; in the case of Socrates there is fortunately a way out of it, if we are careful to interpret our evidence in the light of certain sound general principles.

To begin with the question of the worth of the testimony of Aristophanes and his brother comedians. We have in the first place to remember that the Old Attic Comedy dealt throughout in personal burlesque, not in satire on generalized social "types," and that it was essential to the comedian's success that the object of the burlesque should be a public notoriety. We may therefore be perfectly certain that Socrates was already a well-known figure when Aristophanes attacked him, and that the poet counted upon the excellence of the caricature as something which the audience would recognize. Also we have to remember the general principle that a successful burlesque must be founded on notorious fact, or what is believed to be such.[1] It must be a distortion, for comic effect, of something

[1] The *Clouds* was not a success on the stage, though we see from the allusions to it in Plato's *Apology* that it was already famous as literature at the end of Socrates' life. But the reason for its original ill-success is fairly indicated by Aristophanes himself in our extant version of the play; it contains neither horse-play nor bawdry.

which is not the mere invention of the carica-
turist. Consequently, when Aristophanes makes
it the main point of his play to represent Socrates
as the head of something like a regular "School"
who combine physical science with what we
should call "spiritualism," though we should be
very foolish if we took his representations at anything like their "face value," we should be equally
foolish not to ask ourselves what are the real
facts which explain the caricature, and whether
we cannot discern them reappearing from a different angle of vision in what we are told by
Plato or Xenophon.

It is true, again, that there is a marked contrast
between the Socrates of the Aristophanic play,
with his "pupils" and "thinking-shop," and the
Platonic (or Xenophontic) Socrates with his
"mission" to every one who will listen to him.
But when we remember that Aristophanes is bur-
lesquing Socrates as he was, or was believed to
be, at a time when Plato and Xenophon were
little more than babies, we should see that the
contrast may well be largely explained by this
difference in date. It may prove to be the fact
that Socrates at forty-five was in some ways a
different man from Socrates at fifty-five or sixty,
and that evidence of the fact is actually supplied
by the works of Plato and Xenophon themselves,

when we read them with proper attention. I shall accordingly make use, for the purpose of this sketch, of the evidence of Attic comedy, though, I hope, always with due caution.

When we come to consider the real or alleged discrepancies between Plato and Xenophon themselves, the first thing that is likely to strike us is that they have often been unduly exaggerated. Except on one or two points of detail, Xenophon does not formally contradict anything which Plato tells us about Socrates. What he does is to leave things out, or to reduce them to the level of the commonplace. The range of information with which he supplies us is limited. It is possible, using Plato alone, to compile a rather full biography of his hero, from early manhood to the last years; it would be quite impossible to construct any such narrative from the much more meagre information supplied by Xenophon,[1] though careful reading will often show us that he incidentally confirms some of Plato's most characteristic assertions. Again, the vivid individuality of Plato's portrait of Socrates is all but entirely lost in Xenophon, who ignores most of the pecu-

[1] I have tried to make this clear in detail in an article in the *Proceedings of the British Academy* for 1917–1918 (pp. 93 ff.) entitled "Plato's Biography of Socrates."

liarities which make Plato's hero an "original."
The "irony," or peculiar humour, of Socrates, for
example, and his characteristic attitude of "Socratic doubt" are both known to us exclusively
from Plato; Xenophon's Socrates has no doubts
about anything and no humour to speak of. Now
it is, of course, a possible explanation of this that
Socrates was a commonplace person whom Plato
has converted into a first-rate figure by crediting
him with a personality which really belongs to
Plato himself.[1] But it is also an equally possible
hypothesis that the actual man Socrates had the
marvellous endowments Plato ascribes to him,
and that their absence from the slighter sketch of
Xenophon is due to imperfect insight, or lack of
dramatic power in the author. The commonplace
personality may be that of the writer, not that
of his subject. We have also to bear in mind that
the avowed purpose of Xenophon's *Memorials*
requires him to present Socrates in a commonplace light. Though the book lacks thorough-
going unity of design, and was clearly composed
piecemeal, its general character is determined by

[1] More than one excellent work on Plato is, for example, vitiated by the assumption that the wonderful
picture of Socrates drawn in the *Symposium* is psychological self-revelation on the part of Plato. Whether it
is really that or not, at least that is not what it professes
to be.

the fact that it opens as a formal *apology*, or defence, for Socrates against the charges made
against him at his trial. Xenophon's object is to
argue that, on their own premisses, the dicasts
who found Socrates guilty of irreligion and misleading "the young" were making a mistake; he
was really a model of all that his prosecutors
themselves understood by piety, and the morality
he practised and inculcated was exactly what the
ordinary good Athenian citizen would desire to
exhibit in his own life and impress on his sons, if
he could. Now it is, of course, clear, as Burnet
has said, that such a defence fails precisely because
it is too successful; if Socrates had been what
Xenophon wants us to believe, he would never
have been prosecuted. Xenophon's apologetic
purpose absolutely requires him to suppress, as
far as he can, any feature in the character of his
hero which is original, and therefore disconcerting to a dull and conventionally-minded reader.
It follows that in reading his narrative we must
never forget the principle, which applies to all
polemic of this kind, that the most valuable statements of the apologist are just those incidental
admissions which are incompatible with the case
he is putting forward. For example, Xenophon is
damaging his own case when he incidentally be-
trays in one passage the fact that Socrates had at

some date been something very like the head of
a group of scientific students,[1] in another that he
possessed advanced knowledge of geometry and
astronomy,[2] and in a third that foreign Pythagoreans were among his intimate associates[3]; and
this gives a peculiar significance to his evidence
on all these points. Even if we suppose that
Xenophon is here drawing upon Platonic dialogues such as the *Phaedo*, which he had certainly
read, that he should do so is proof that he found
Plato's representations consistent with what he
knew of Socrates. If we read Xenophon in the
light of the cautions just given, I believe it will
be found that his account of the philosopher nowhere seriously contradicts the fuller Platonic
narrative, and at times confirms it in a remarkable
way.

We still have to face the main objection which
has been brought against the Platonic dialogues
as a faithful representation of the life and thought
of a real historical person. It is clear that without
Plato we have no material for a connected biography of Socrates which will throw any light on
his personality; it is also true that Plato offers us
a very full, vivid, and internally consistent picture of the central personage of his dialogues.
But this, of itself, does not prove that Plato's

[1]*Mem.*, I. vi. 14.   [2]*Mem.*, IV. vii. 2–6.   [3]*Mem.*, I. ii. 48.

Socrates may not be, from first to last, a product
of the creative imagination, like Othello or Fal-
staff, and it is still held in many quarters, though
not so confidently as it was held fifty years ago,
that he is this. Can we give any sufficient reason
for rejecting this once generally accepted belief?
To argue the point exhaustively would require
an entire volume, but I may indicate here the
main considerations which seem to my own mind
decisive.[1]

In the first place, the minute researches of
scholars of the last fifty or sixty years, Lewis
Campbell, C. Ritter, Lutoslawski, and others, have
definitely proved that a certain group of important Platonic dialogues (*Sophistes*, *Politicus*,
Philebus, *Timaeus*, *Laws*), with marked pecu-
liarities of vocabulary and style, must be later
than the rest of the philosopher's writings, and

[1] In the absence of such a volume I would refer the
reader in the first instance to certain works of Professor Burnet, especially the article "Socrates" in Hastings' *Encyclopaedia of Religion and Ethics*, vol. xi; the
Introduction to his edition of the *Phaedo* (Oxford,
1911); and *Greek Philosophy*, Pt. i, *Thales to Plato*
(1914), c. 8, "The Life of Socrates." I would add a
further reference to the recent excellent little *Sokrates*
of the eminent Platonic scholar, Constantin Ritter
(Tübingen, 1931). Among earlier works, Ivo Bruns,
Das literarische Porträt der Griechen (1896), is particularly good.

clearly belong to an advanced period of his life in which he was the head of an organized school with a very definite doctrine of its own. It is clear that these works were written at a much later period of life than the great mass of Plato's dialogues, and among this larger mass there are one or two, *Republic*, *Phaedrus*, *Theaetetus*, which seem to be, in point of style, transitional. There is consequently a general consensus of scholars that the greater number of the Platonic dialogues must have been composed before Plato had definitely founded his school, the Academy; the *Sophistes–Laws* group after the Academy had definitely established itself as an organized institution; the works of the transitional period either about the time of its first foundation or during the first decades of its existence.[1] Now, whereas in all earlier dialogues Socrates is always

[1] The precise date of the foundation of the Academy, the first European University, is not known, but it cannot have been before Plato's fortieth year (388/7 B.C.), and can hardly have been much later. The *Theaetetus* has been fairly shown to have been written about 368 B.C., and is certainly the latest of the "transitional" group, as the *Republic* is the earliest. (Personally I agree with those who hold that the *Republic* must have been substantially written either just before the foundation of the Academy or within a few years of the foundation.) The "late" dialogues from *Sophistes* to *Laws* are pretty certainly all subsequent to 360 B.C.

the central figure and the leader of discussion, we find that this is completely changed in the group which opens with the *Sophistes*. In only one of these latest dialogues (the *Philebus*, which discusses questions of ethics and moral psychology) is Socrates the leading person. In the *Sophistes*, *Politicus*, *Timaeus* he is present, but takes no part in the discussion, and in the *Laws* he is left out altogether. The logical and political doctrines of *Sophistes* and *Politicus* are expounded by an unnamed visitor from Elea, the physical theories of the *Timaeus* by an Italian Pythagorean, and the vast scheme of jurisprudence of the *Laws* by an anonymous Athenian. I can see no reason for this remarkable change of method but that given by Burnet, that Plato's historical sense forbade him to make Socrates the expositor of philosophical and scientific interests and doctrines which Plato well knew to be his own and those of his contemporaries. Here we have, as I think, positive proof that Plato did not use the figure of Socrates as a "mask" for himself or as an imaginary ideal of what "the philosopher" should be. If he had done so, there is no intelligible reason why the game should not have been kept up indefinitely. We may fairly infer that Plato was at least unconscious of any departure from historical verisimilitude in the picture drawn of Socrates in the more numerous dialogues where that philosopher is the central figure.[1]

In the next place, there is one group among Plato's early writings where any other purpose seems to be excluded, those which deal with the circumstances of the trial and death of Socrates (*Euthyphro, Apology, Crito, Phaedo*). The case was a *cause célèbre*, as we can see from the strictures of Isocrates in his *Busiris* on the *littérateur* Polycrates and the pamphlet in which he presented the argument for the prosecution. It is certain that Plato's *Apology* must have been circulated within a very few years of the trial, and must have been read by many of the actual judges

[1] One should note in this connection the remarkable passage, *Timaeus*, 19 *b* ff., where Socrates is made to confess his own inability to depict the conduct of a State engaged in the activities of war or diplomacy, and appears to ascribe this deficiency to his want of political experience. There is nothing in the *Republic* itself like this sense of the limitations of Socrates. The reappearance of Socrates as the leading figure in the *Philebus* is explained by the fact that the questions dealt with there are at bottom the same as those which had been treated in earlier dialogues like the *Gorgias*. Of course it is not suggested that all Plato's Socratic dialogues are close reports of actual conversations, like those recorded by Boswell, though it is likely enough that some of them are founded on actual conversations. What is meant is simply that the dialogues intend to exhibit a faithful picture of the situation, interests, and views of a real historical man.

as well as by many who had been among the
audience. A misrepresentation under such conditions would have been suicidal for its author, and
we should infer that the very characteristic "defence"—in fact, a defiance—which Plato puts into
the mouth of his Master is, in its main features,
a reproduction of what was actually said. So
much is, indeed, now admitted by most of the
scholars whose names carry most weight (*e.g.*
Ritter and Wilamowitz-Moellendorff). But I
think, with Burnet, that we are bound in consistency to go a step further. The same considerations apply with equal force to the *Phaedo*, with
its description of the last hours of the life of
Socrates. Plato tells us that he was himself absent
from the scene through illness, but we know,
on the testimony of one of his own personal
scholars,[1] that he and the other members of the
Socratic circle actually passed the weeks immediately after the execution at Megara, in the
company of the philosopher Euclides, who is one
of the characters of the narrative. Thus there can
be no doubt that Plato must have been minutely
informed on the events of that memorable day

---

[1] Hermodorus, who is quoted for the fact in D. L.,
iii. 6: "Then, at the age of twenty-eight, he [Plato]
with other Socratics withdrew to Euclides at Megara."
(The same statement is also made, *ib.*, ii. 106.)

by a number of eye-witnesses. It is certain also that many, if not all, of the persons introduced into the dialogue as spectators or interlocutors were living when the *Phaedo* was circulated (for example, Euclides himself and Simmias, one of the main interlocutors). It is inconceivable to me that Plato could have perpetuated a mystification on such a theme, even if he had wished to do so, in the face of certain detection. And unless the *Phaedo* is a deliberate mystification, it follows at once that its central doctrine, the so-called "Theory of Ideas," which is represented as adopted by Socrates in his youth and familiar to all his auditors, really was a Socratic tenet, and is no discovery of Plato's. If this is so, the supposed reason for believing that Plato took liberties with historical truth in these dialogues vanishes, and there is nothing to prevent us from accepting the view of them most directly suggested by their contents—that their immediate purpose is not to propound a doctrine personal to their writer, but to preserve the memory of a great thinker and of a great age which had left no literature of its own.[1]

[1] It is not true, as is sometimes supposed, that Aristotle ever says that the "Theory of Ideas" was unknown to Socrates, though even if he had said this, it would be no more than an inference of his own. What is true is that Aristotle usually connects the theory with the names of

The truth seems to be, in fact, that Plato, like Kant, is one of those philosophers whose most characteristic personal positions are only attained in late middle age. Before he was a philosopher with a doctrine and a school of his own, he was a great dramatic artist, and used his dramatic gifts to make Socrates and his circle live for a generation to whom they would, without him, have been little more than names. When he wrote these great dramatic dialogues he had probably as yet no "doctrine" of his own; by the time he had a Platonic philosophy to impart, his dramatic power had been enfeebled. We must bear in mind that Plato, to all appearance, was the inventor of the Socratic dialogue as a literary form.[1] It is not

Plato and his followers, and that in one passage (*Metaphysics*, 1078 *b* 11), where he speaks of "those who had first said that there are Forms (or Ideas)," he may be referring to Plato (though this is not certain). Since the theory was certainly introduced into philosophical *literature* by the Socratic dialogues of Plato, such an expression would in any case be natural. The statement of the *Nicomachean Ethics* that the theory was introduced by "friends" of Aristotle (*E.N.*, 1096 *a* 13) proves nothing. A doctrine of Socrates would be one held in a quarter which any disciple of Plato might speak of as "friendly."

[1] It is certain, or all but certain, that all the Socratic writings of Xenophon are later than most of the "Socratic" dialogues of Plato. The same thing *appears* to be true, so far as can be discovered, of the dialogues of Aeschines.

clear why he should have chosen such a method of utterance if his purpose had been primarily to inculcate his own philosophy. For that purpose, dialogues between well-known persons of a generation before the writer's own would have been a very unsatisfactory vehicle. But if Plato's purpose was primarily to keep alive the memory of a great man and a great age, we see at once why he chose to invent the particular literary form most specially appropriate to his object.

It has been asked why Plato should have composed so many and such elaborate works if the thought enshrined in them is in all its main features that of other persons. The obvious reason is that he was living, as he well knew, in a "post-war" society which had survived its own day of greatness. To recreate in imagination the chief thinker of the great days of the fifth century and the circle in which he moved was at once a duty of piety to Socrates, to the perished splendours of Athens, and incidentally to the famous Athenian family to which Plato belonged, and a refuge from the personal heart-break to which Plato's *Seventh Epistle* testifies. It is too often forgotten that without the evidence of Plato's Socratic dialogues we should really know nothing at all to speak of about the intellectual life of the sixty years or so from the repulse of Xerxes to the Peace of Nicias, just the most vital and splendid period of Attic history.[1] Historians, as a matter of fact, habitually draw on these dialogues for their picture of the intellectual movements of this great age, but they would lose their right to do so if Plato could be suspected of playing fast and loose with historical truth, as he is often alleged to have done in his statements about Socrates.[2] A theory of his literary methods which its own adherents are constantly driven to ignore is hardly likely to be a sound one.

The assumption upon which the following account of Socrates will be based is, then, that Plato's picture of his Master is substantially accurate, and that the information he supplies about him is intended to be taken as historical fact. It does not, of course, follow that there has been no "transfiguration" of Socrates in Plato's mind by meditation on his death as a martyr, but it does follow that any such process of idealization

[1] This point is made with special effect in the posthumous volume of Burnet, *Platonism* (University of California Press, 1928), pp. 5 ff.

[2] Every historian who makes statements about the "Sophistic age" is dependent for most of what he says on Platonic dialogues like the *Protagoras* and *Gorgias*, though a writer who regards Plato's Socrates as a fictitious personage ought in consistency to take the same view of his Protagoras or Gorgias or Thrasymachus.

has been unconscious, and that there is no deliberate mystification in the dialogues. It does not
follow, again, that everything Plato tells us must
be precise historical truth. When he is describing
Socrates, as he often does, as he was in the days
of his own boyhood (as in the *Symposium*), or
even long before his own birth (as in the *Parmenides*), he is speaking of matters of which he
could have no personal knowledge, and is liable
to possible mistake about them. But we have to
remember that, by his own account, members of
his family, from his maternal great-grandfather,
the Critias of the *Timaeus*, down to his uncle
Charmides and his two elder brothers, had all
been more or less intimate with Socrates. He
would thus be in a position to be exceptionally
well informed about a great deal which fell outside the range of his own memories.[1] If the results

[1]Xenophon also must be depending on the testimony
of older men for what we shall find to be the most
illuminating things which he tells us. But in his case we
have not the same reasons as we have in Plato's for
feeling confidence in the competence of his informants.
The only informant whom he names, Hermogenes, the
half-brother of the wealthy Callias, does not strike one
in the pictures drawn of him by Plato (in the *Cratylus*)
and Xenophon himself (in his *Symposium*) as a man of
much discretion. It has been probably inferred that
another informant was Antisthenes, who was pretty
certainly an older man than either Xenophon or Plato,
but there is no evidence that Xenophon had any special

obtained by the use of the assumption are internally self-consistent and found to be confirmed at critical points by other evidence, we may fairly regard them as beyond reasonable doubt.

---

opportunity of communication with Antisthenes when he was engaged in the composition of his own "Socratic" works, and it is hardly likely that he had. Modern speculations about possible borrowings in Xenophon from the *writings* of Antisthenes are, of course, only speculations.

argument for historical accuracy of plato.

1. Cessation of use of Socrates in later dialogues where the doctrine is clearly not Socrate's - reflecting respect for historicity

2. Possibility of exposure of falsehood by those many who had known Socrates.

3. Use of dialogue form as opposed to some other - used easily to portray characters but with difficulty to present philosophy.

4. The opportunity of escape avoided by recreation of a character from a happier day

II

THE EARLY LIFE OF SOCRATES

As there was no official registration of births at
Athens, we have no direct record of the birth of
Socrates, son of Sophroniscus and Phaenarete, of
the Antiochid tribe, and the *deme*, or, as we
should say, parish, or ward, of Alopece. Indirectly, however, we can fix the year of his birth
within very narrow limits. There was, of course,
an official record of his trial and condemnation,
which fell in the spring of the year 399 B.C. (the
"year of Laches"), and Plato has told us that
at the time of the trial he was seventy, or rather
older.[1] Hence we shall be very nearly right if we
assume him to have been born in the year 470,
only nine years after the decisive repulse of the
Persian army at Plataea. Thus, when Socrates was

---

[1] *Apology*, 17 *d*. The MSS. vary here between
"seventy" and "over seventy." At *Crito*, 52 *e* 3, Socrates
is made to give his age as "seventy."

born, Pericles was still a very young man, Sophocles and Euripides were lads; Aeschylus had produced his great drama of patriotism, the *Persians*, some two years before, at the charges of Pericles. The philosopher might have been present as a boy at the performance of the *Agamemnon*, and have witnessed every one of the great tragedies of Sophocles and Euripides. All the noble buildings and works of art with which Athens was enriched in the Periclean age, the Long Walls which connected the city with the port of Piraeus, the Parthenon, the statues of Phidias, the frescoes of Polygnotus, were begun and completed under his eyes. The confederacy of Delos, the germ of the Athenian maritime empire, had been formed less than ten years before his birth; he must already have been old enough to be beginning to take notice of what was happening around him when the foundations of Periclean democracy were laid by the ostracism of Pericles' rival Cimon, son of Miltiades (461 B.C.), and the institution of public pay for the democratic jury-courts. He was already a young man of twenty-four or twenty-five when Athens and Sparta concluded the "thirty years' peace," which left Athens, at the price of abandoning her aspirations to dominion on land, free to consolidate her control over the Aegean and to become the first naval power in the world. He was already on the verge of forty at the outbreak of the long war which was to end in the destruction of Athenian greatness. It is important to remember these facts for a very simple reason. The picture of Socrates which has inevitably dominated the imagination of all later ages is that drawn by Plato in the dialogues which deal with his trial and death as an old man, just as the picture which we all have in our minds when we think of Johnson is that of Boswell, who never saw him until he was close on fifty-four and had all the struggles of a life-time behind him. We cannot even begin to understand Socrates historically until we are clear on the point that his youth and early manhood were spent in a society sundered from that in which Plato and Xenophon grew up by the same sort of gulf which divides "post-war" from "pre-war" Europe.

We do not know much about the parents of Socrates. Plato tells us in the *Laches*[1] that Sophroniscus was connected by ties of close friendship with the family of his famous fellow-demesman the "just" Aristides, and implies that he was a man of some consideration in the deme. In the *Crito*[2] it is implied that he was conscientiously careful to give his son the recognized

[1] 180 d.   [2] 50 d.

elementary education in "gymnastic" and music. Phaenarete—the name seems to indicate that she was a woman of good family—had, by another husband, a son named Patrocles[1]; Plato tells us in the *Theaetetus*[2] that she had high skill as an *accoucheuse*. (The statement has sometimes been regarded as a pleasantry, but there seems to be no point in it if it is an invention, and we are not, of course, to commit the anachronism of supposing that Phaenarete was a *professional* midwife.[3]) The Alexandrian tradition, still commonly repeated as fact, is that Sophroniscus was a craftsman, a statuary, or stone-cutter, and we know from both Pausanias[4] and Diogenes Laertius[5] that in the second century A.D. a group of the Graces on the Acropolis was shown as the work of Socrates himself. This, however, seems very doubtful. Archaeologists seem to be agreed that the

---

[1]Plato, *Euthydemus*, 297 e.   [2]149 a.

[3]Plato's point is that Socrates jestingly compares the services he renders to his young friends by helping them to "deliver themselves" of ideas with the skill of his mother. That Socrates really did speak in this way seems to be proved by the fact that in the *Clouds*, a play produced when Plato was an infant, Aristophanes has a joke about the "miscarriage of a notion" (*Clouds*, 137). This would be silly unless it is a parody of some way of speaking the audience would recognize as characteristically Socratic.

[4]I. xxii. 8.   [5]ii. 19.

group described by Pausanias must belong to a sculptor of an earlier period (the name Socrates was a common one). The earliest extant reference to Socrates as the son of a worker in stone is found in some satiric lines quoted from the third-century verse-writer Timon of Phlius, and, as Burnet has said, it seems at least plain that neither Plato nor Xenophon had ever heard anything of the story. If Plato had known it, he would hardly have made Socrates say, as he does in the *Apology*, that when he set himself to look round for a wiser man than himself he began at once with the politicians, turned next to the poets, and only explored the "artisans" last. I think with Burnet that the statement probably arose from a misunderstanding of a playful reference by Socrates in Plato[1] to Daedalus, the legendary maker of wooden images, as his ancestor, and that the true meaning of this jest is that the family had a pedigree which traced their line back to Daedalus, exactly as the house of the Philaidae, to which Pisistratus and Alcibiades belonged, traced their origin to Aeacus. In any case, it seems plain that if Plato is to be trusted, Socrates himself had

[1] Plato, *Euthyphro*, 10 *c*. This seems certainly to be the way in which the connection with Daedalus was understood by the writer of [Plat.] *Alcibiades I.* 121 *a*. It is not a sufficient objection that we have no other evidence of a clan of Daedalidae.

never followed any craft. He is depicted as
always having had absolute leisure to occupy
himself as his tastes directed, and as having con-
sorted from the first with the most distinguished
men of Athens, the circles of Pericles and Cimon.

Whether Sophroniscus was a statuary or not,
we must not make the mistake of thinking of
Socrates as belonging to a needy class, like the
modern "proletariat." He was extremely poor in
his old age—after a disastrous war which resulted
in a general "financial crisis"—but Plato makes a
point of it that this poverty was directly due to
absorption in a "mission" which left no time for
attendance to "personal affairs."[1] Down to his
forty-sixth year, at any rate, he cannot have belonged to the poorest class of Athenian citizens,
as he was still serving in 424 as a "hoplite" or
fully-armed infantryman, and must have been
officially credited with the income which ren-
dered him liable to this service. The prominence
given to his alleged neediness in the burlesques
produced the year after by the comic poets suggests, though it does not absolutely prove, that
his impoverishment was then recent. Hence there
seems some reason to believe a statement of the
third-century scholar Demetrius of Phalerum[2]
that Socrates inherited, besides a dwelling-house,

[1] *Apology*, 23 c.   [2] Plutarch, *Aristides*, 1.

a modest capital (seventy *minae*), which was invested for him by his friend Crito.

From his earliest days, Socrates must have been something of what we call an "oddity," both physically and mentally. His physical robustness and powers of endurance are dwelt upon by both Plato and Xenophon, and partly explain the excellence of his record as a fighting-man. It is further testimony to his physical vigour that when he died at the age of seventy he left two small children, one of whom appears to have been an infant in arms.[1] Stress is laid upon his exceptional continence and abstemiousness in eating and drinking, and also upon his power, on appropriate occasions, of drinking deep without being affected by the winecup. In his manhood he used to wear the same single garment winter and summer, and habitually went barefoot, even, according to Plato, in the rigours of a winter campaign.[2] But he was very far from being hand-

[1] At least we are told in the *Phaedo* (60 *a*) that when the friends of Socrates were admitted to the prison on the last day of his life they found his wife Xanthippe already there "with the child." Xanthippe presumably had spent the night there, and had brought the child as too young to be left at home.

[2] See the description of his hardihood in the frozen trenches before Potidaea, Plato, *Symp.*, 220 *a–b*. Amipsias described him in the *Connus* (423 B.C.) as "born

some or well-made. Aristophanes compared his walk to the strut of a waterfowl, and made fun of his habit of rolling his eyes; Plato and Xenophon both allude to the breadth of his nostrils and the marked snubness of his nose, as well as to some peculiarity of his eyes, which may be either their prominence or the breadth of the space between them.[1] He looked, says Alcibiades in Plato's *Symposium*, like some grotesque, a satyr or a Silenus.

Mentally, also, Socrates was in more than one way singular. His most striking singularity was the mysterious "voice" or "supernatural sign,"[2] which attended him from the days of his childhood. According to Plato, who treats the peculiarity very lightly, the "sign" manifested itself sporadically, often on very trivial occasions, and always took the form of a sudden inhibition[3];

---

to spite the shoemakers." For Aristophanes' description see *Clouds*, 362 ff.

[1] Compare the accounts of Plato, *Symp.*, 215 *b* ff., and Xenophon, *Symp.* 5.

[2] This is what later writers call the "daemon" or "guardian spirit" of Socrates. Plato never speaks of it in this way. He calls it simply "the supernatural sign," or "the supernatural something." See the full account of it given by Socrates himself to his judges, *Apology*, 31 *d*.

[3] At *Rep.*, 496 *c*, Socrates speaks of the "sign" as a personal peculiarity of which his own is probably the one unique case.

experience showed that neglect of its warnings commonly led to unpleasant consequences. Xenophon, who had a vein of superstition in his own character, makes rather more of this oddity, which he treats as a kind of private oracle, and insists that it also gave positive directions, which it was not safe to neglect, for the actions of both Socrates and his friends. The fourth-century dialogue *Theages*, wrongly attributed to Plato, contains a number of striking anecdotes about persons who had disregarded warnings given by the "sign," always with disastrous consequences. Plato's version of the thing, as the least sensational, is likely to be the most accurate. It is clear from all the accounts that the "sign" was nothing of the nature of "conscience." It had nothing to do with right and wrong, and is never appealed to, in any of the accounts of it, on points of moral conduct, but amounts to a sort of "uncanny" *flair* for bad luck. Its chief interest for us is that it is one indication among others that Socrates really possessed the temperament of the "visionary," though, unlike most seers of visions, he kept that side of his nature well in check, as St. Paul did his gift for "speaking with tongues." Another mark of the visionary temperament dwelt on by Plato is his liability to sudden fits of absorption and abstraction, amounting at times to actual trance or "ecstasy." These were apparently usually of brief duration, but Plato records one which befell the philosopher as he was serving before Potidaea, and lasted the whole of a day and a night.[1] Facts of this kind throw a light on the strong vein of mysticism which is characteristic of Plato's Socratic dialogues. This is commonly interpreted as evidence for the presence of a mystical tendency in Plato himself, but in view of the marked elimination of this strain from the later dialogues in which Socrates has ceased to be prominent, it seems more reasonable to infer that the mysticism of such works as the *Symposium* and *Phaedrus* belongs in the first instance to Socrates—a point to which we shall have to recur later on.

What curbed this vein and prevented it from developing, in the case of Socrates, into superstition was, according to Plato, not only the "obstinate rationality" which he shared with Samuel Johnson, but the shrewd humour in which he also resembled the "sage" of Fleet Street. It is this humour which his opponents in Plato's dialogues speak of as his "habitual irony." Irony, in

[1] The *Symposium* describes Socrates as overtaken by a brief "rapt" of this kind on his way to a dinner-party (*Symp.*, 174 *d*). In the same dialogue (220 *c–d*) the scene before Potidaea is described by Alcibiades, who had been a witness of it.

this, the primitive sense of the word, means the disagreeable characteristic of the man who contrives to evade his responsibilities by an affected disparagement of his abilities.[1] Socrates is accused by his unfavourable critics in Plato of this affectation because he habitually represents himself as the humble inquirer who wants to sit at the feet of those who know more than himself, while it is manifest that he is really their intellectual superior. Hence his disclaimers are taken as uncandid excuses for confining himself to the easy task of exposing the deficiencies of other men. Plato's own conviction, of course, is that Socrates' professions are perfectly serious. He declares himself ignorant for the same reason that he thinks very little of the wisdom upon which some of his contemporaries plume themselves: he has a sound and exacting standard of what real knowledge should be, and therefore knows how far short he and all the rest of them come of reaching that standard. Hence he alone sees both

[1]The typical "ironist" of the animal world, in the language of Greek fable, is Reynard the Fox. The "ironical man" of Aristotle's *Ethics* is the man whose conversation is made offensive by the affectation of mock-humility, insincere depreciation of himself and everything connected with himself. Both his pose and that of the braggart are contrasted by Aristotle with the straightforward veracity of the man who is candid and free from "self-consciousness."

himself and the rest of mankind in their true proportions, and the contrast between men's pretensions and their performance appeals to his sense of humour.

The almost universal adoption of symbolic language borrowed from sexual passion by the mystics of all times and places seems to point to a real connection between the mystical and the erotic temperament. Socrates was clearly no exception to this rule, and it is a consequence of the manners of the fashionable circles of his age that his imagery is borrowed from the vocabulary of romantic attachment between persons of the same sex. The most striking example is afforded by what is said in Plato about the famous association between him and his brilliant fellow-citizen Alcibiades, a man somewhere between fifteen and twenty years younger than himself.[1] This attachment, which must date from a time when Alcibiades was a mere boy and Socrates a man in his thirties, is described by Plato in the language of romantic passion, and Plato is confirmed on the point by a still surviving sentence put into the mouth of Socrates by Aeschines in his dia-

---

[1] See in particular *Protagoras*, 309 *a*, *Gorgias*, 481 *d*, and, above all, the narrative put into the mouth of Alcibiades himself, *Symp.*, 217 *a*–219 *d*.

logue *Alcibiades*.[1] Xenophon is naturally silent
about the attachment of Socrates to Alcibiades,
which, as we shall see, was one of the principal
counts against him in the mind of the democratic
politicians who brought him to trial, but he agrees
with Plato's representation that it was Socrates'
habit to speak of himself playfully as a lifelong
victim of Eros and a master in the *ars amoris*.[2]
Both Plato and Xenophon make it perfectly clear
that this language was playful, and we must be
careful not to misunderstand it. The absolute
moral purity of Socrates is the presupposition of
the story of his "temptation" put into the mouth
of Alcibiades himself in the *Symposium*, and the
whole object of the treatment of the subject in
Plato's two great "erotic" dialogues, *Symposium*
and *Phaedrus*, is to disentangle the *amor mysticus*
from sensual or sentimental corruptions.[3]

[1]See the words of Aeschines' *Alcibiades*, Fr. 4
(Krauss), where Socrates is made to compare his "love"
(ἔρως) for Alcibiades with the Bacchic "possession."

[2]Apart from frequent allusions of this kind in Plato, cf.
the playful assertions to the same effect in Xenophon,
Symp., viii. 2, *Mem.*, III. xi. 16 ff.

[3]It may be worth while to remark that the "corruption of the young" with which Socrates was charged has
nothing to do with this side of his relation to his juniors.
It is certain both that an imputation of "homosexuality"
would have been an effective weapon in the hands of his
accusers, and that no such imputation was made by

We have to think of Socrates in his early manhood, then, as an original genius in whose character there was a unique blend of the passionate lover, the religious mystic, the eager rationalist, and the humorist; we are to reconstruct, as far as we can on the strength of the surviving records, the reaction upon such a character of the intense intellectual life of the Periclean age. The task is a hazardous one, but I believe it can be accomplished if we trust to indications given us by Plato, and interpret our other evidence in the light of them.

In one respect, indeed, we have probably to reckon with an influence from a still earlier generation. The Socrates of the Platonic dialogues frequently refers to the dogmas of the Orphic religion as supporting his own convictions about the immortality of the soul and the importance of the life to come, and the details of the imaginative myths which he relates about Heaven and Hell in the *Gorgias*, *Phaedo*, *Republic*, are notoriously Orphic. Plato, too, as we see from allusions in the *Laws*, regarded "ancient sayings,"

---

them. The real charge, as we shall see, was that of "educating" Alcibiades and Critias, and so being responsible for their offences against the democracy. I only mention the obvious point because it has been quite lately grossly misrepresented in an article in the *Quarterly Review*.

which plainly mean the Orphic doctrines, as fables with a kernel of imperishable religious truth; but we see also from the unsparing attack on immoral mythology and religion in the second book of the *Republic*, which is aimed much more at Orpheus than at Homer, that it was Plato's view that by the time of his own birth[1] Orphicism had degenerated into vulgar trafficking in "pardons" and "indulgences." Contemporary Orphicism is not likely, therefore, to have inspired either Plato or Socrates with respect. Pindar's greatest Orphic odes, however, belong to the years just before Socrates' birth, and this suggests the probability that Socrates really had been initiated in the Orphic religion in childhood[2] and permanently impressed by it. That fact, if it is a

[1] The conversation which the *Republic* proposes to describe must be imagined to take place at the latest in Plato's early childhood, if not earlier, since his eldest brother, Adimantus, who figures there as a young man, was old enough to stand *in loco parentis* to him in 399, as we see from *Apology*, 34 *a*, where Socrates mentions him as a relative who could be trusted to give an authoritative opinion on the effect of his own society upon Plato.

[2] It must be remembered that the Orphic religion was not that of any political community. It was recruited, like a modern church, by voluntary initiation in its sacraments, and was "international." The original Pythagoreans combined a similar religion based on the doctrine of the immortal soul with their science.

fact, will contribute to account for the standing
connection which we shall find between Socrates
and the Pythagoreans of Thebes and Phlius, as
well as for Plato's obvious anxiety in the dialogue
Euthyphro to exhibit the difference between the
piety of Socrates and that of the fantastic sectary
Euthyphron, and for the existence of a dialogue
Telauges by Aeschines, in which Socrates was
brought into company with an "other-worldly"
devotee of particularly dirty habits, and apparently made to criticize his ways.

It was, no doubt, from the spirit of Periclean
Athens that Socrates derived the lifelong sense
of the importance of implicit obedience to lawful
authority and the reverence for strict constitu-
tionality which led him in later life to oppose
violation of the constitution, alike by the angry
democracy and by its subverters, at grave personal risk, and, in the end, to submit to a trial
which it was intended by his accusers he should
evade, and a sentence from which he might easily
have escaped, in vindication of the right of the
State to pronounce on the conduct of its citizens.
His whole life was a signal example of that
reverence for law which we are accustomed to
think Roman rather than Greek, and yet singu-
larly free from the besetting Roman vice of exalt-
ing the mere letter of the law above its spirit.

More needs to be said about the intellectual atmosphere of the society in which Socrates passed his youth and earlier manhood, and its influence upon him. The important fact we have to keep before our minds is that the rise of Athens to political and commercial importance in the time of Cimon and Pericles had made it, like London in our own days, a great capital and a place of resort for the thinkers of the Hellenic world. It had become a kind of "clearing-house" for ideas of all kinds. This is why, in the next century, Plato could establish at Athens an Academy which became an "international" centre of higher education, and why when we hear of the science and philosophy of the ancient Greeks we think at once of the "schools of Athens," though, in fact, philosophy and science originated outside Athens and were so uncongenial to the Athenian character that Socrates and Plato themselves are the only Athenian philosophers of any note.

Philosophy and science, as yet undiscriminated from one another, had been the creation of the intellectual curiosity of the Greeks of the Great Ionian cities of the seaboard of Asia Minor, who set themselves, from somewhere about 600 B.C. onwards, to construct a rational and coherent theory of the world around them. Within a couple of generations of the origination of the intellectual movement, the impulse had been carried to the Greek Societies of Southern Italy by one of the greatest of the Ionian men of genius, Pythagoras, the real founder of mathematics, with the result that the West became rapidly still more important than the East for the future development of European thought. The primary interest of the original Ionian men of science had been in the "things above us," the heavenly bodies which seem to move in a way which is at once complex and baffling and yet regulated by some uniform law, if only we could discover what that law is. The rise of Greek medicine had then led to a displacement of astronomical by biological speculation as the dominating influence in the "scientific world," while mathematics had attained a high degree of development and had suggested to the Pythagoreans the thought that the science of number itself is probably the key to the secrets of the universe.[1] By the time that Socrates was

[1] The English reader will find the most satisfactory general sketch of the whole development down to *c.* 450 B.C. in Burnet's *Greek Philosophy*, Pt. 1, pp. 1–101. Further details may be studied in the same author's *Early Greek Philosophy* (ed. 3, 1920) or P. Tannery, *Pour l'histoire de la science Hellène* (ed. 2, 1930). For a brief account of the early history of mathematics see G. Loria, *Histoire des sciences mathématiques dans l'antiquité Hellénique* (Paris, 1929). It seems clear that

entering on his twenties the Eastern and Western theories of the universe were crystallizing into a certain opposition to one another, of which the most prominent "outward and visible sign" was the different account of the earth's shape and place in the scheme of things given in the two systems. The general Eastern view was that there is a single stuff of which everything, including our own minds, is made. This stuff is "air," and by *air* was meant mist or vapour. Everything is mist or vapour, and the differences between things are due simply to variations in the degree of condensation or rarefaction of this primitive stuff. Even the human "soul" is *air*, being, in fact, just the portion of the surrounding atmosphere which we draw into our bodies by respiration. This is why we only have life and consciousness so long as we continue to breathe, and why we "give up the ghost" when we die. The earth, a large mass of highly-condensed *air* which lies in the centre of our particular "world," or stellar system, is a broad disc which floats on the air beneath it as a leaf floats on the surface of a stream. As this Eastern view was in principle monistic, the rival Western views were in prin-

by the early manhood of Socrates the Greek geometers were in possession of the *substance* of the contents of *Euclid*, i, ii, iii, iv, vi.

ciple dualistic or pluralistic. The best known of
these theories to the average modern reader is
that of Empedocles, the founder of the Sicilian
medical school, who held that so far from being
air in varying states of condensation, all things
are compounds of *four* primitive "roots" (the
elements of a later terminology), fire, atmos-
pheric air, water, "earth." A still more striking
contrast with the Eastern theory is afforded by
the view of the Pythagoreans, who tried to conceive of things in a strictly mathematical way as
so many figures constituted by "units" or
"points," arranged in characteristic geometrical
patterns in a circumambient "space," which was
not clearly discriminated from mist or darkness.
Now the Pythagoreans had discovered the spheri-
cal shape of the earth, and the consequent impossibility of supposing it to float upon any support. They went back to the brilliant idea of
Anaximander, who, though he supposed the earth
to be drum-shaped, had declared in the earliest
days of Ionian science that it is not supported
by anything, but swings free in the centre of the
whole stellar system because it is symmetrically
placed, and there is thus no reason why it should
deviate in one direction rather than in another.
This direct clash between the typically Eastern
and Western views of the shape of the earth is

a good example of the condition of scientific thought in the middle of the fifth century. Science had been zealously pursued for a century and a half, with the result, as Socrates is made to hint in Plato's *Phaedo*, that nothing seemed certain but that if any of its rival exponents were right, all the others must be wrong.[1]

N.B.

Even more disconcerting than the contradictory assertions of the conflicting scientific schools was the radical criticism upon all of them of the Eleatic philosophers, Parmenides and his pupil Zeno. Starting from the rationalist principle that what cannot be thought without self-contradiction cannot be true, Parmenides had declared that motion and change, the fundamental characteristics of the world as described by science, are self-contradictory, and must therefore be illusory. What really is must be a single, uniform, unchanging "Absolute"[2]; since Nature, as envisaged by the cosmologists, is not such an Absolute but a scene of incessant motion and transformation, Nature can only be an illusion. Zeno had carried the war into the heart of the enemy's camp by subjecting the mathematical

[1] 96 *a–b*, 99 *b–c*.

[2] Parmenides thought quite naïvely of this Absolute as a solid material sphere, but this is a mere historical incident.

principles of the Pythagoreans to a searching examination which appeared to prove that mathematical thought itself is a mass of contradictions, and, in fact, led to a reconstruction of mathematical fundamental concepts which began in the age of Plato and has barely been completed in our own.[1] The effect of this apparently unanswerable assault on the first elements of rational knowledge was to produce by the middle of the fifth century B.C. a widespread general scepticism of the very possibility of knowledge of the natural world. By the time that Socrates was a young man of twenty the ablest and most outstanding men were all turning away from the physical world as an object of study; it was almost exclusively the second-rate minds which went on patching up the old systems. The first-rate men, like Protagoras of Abdera, were turning their thoughts in a different direction. In an age of rapid moral and political progress the need was felt for thought-out and clearly formulated principles in legislation, politics, the personal conduct of life, to take the place of reliance on tradition and custom, and here there seemed to be a fruit-

[1] Zeno's famous "paradoxes," *Achilles*, *The Flying Arrow*, and the rest, belong to this polemic. The fullest study of its importance and effects known to me is H. Hasse and H. Scholz, *Die Grundlagenkrisis der Griechischen Mathematik*, Berlin, 1928.

ful opening for employment of intelligence to real purpose. This explains the rise of a new profession, that of the "sophist,"[1] or paid "educator of men." Men who a little while earlier would have been students of Nature found a new and remunerative occupation in travelling from one city to another as professed exponents of "virtue" or "goodness," that is, of the knowledge "how to conduct one's private affairs and the affairs of one's city well," the precise knowledge a youthful aspirant to power and distinction would be most anxious to acquire. The humanistic studies of Europe have their beginning in this movement, as the natural sciences have theirs in the cosmological speculations of the "wise men" of Miletus. The rapid rise of an imperial democracy in Attica in the Periclean age naturally made of Athens a world-capital in which the professor of "goodness" could make sure of an eager audience and a rich harvest.

Both the older interest in mathematical and

[1] The word at this date means simply what our ancestors in the age of Queen Anne called a "wit," and includes theorists about cosmology as well as "humanists." We must not read into it any of the moral disparagement conveyed by our words *sophist* and *sophistry*. Isocrates and Plato between them created these implications by their adoption of the word to mean a counterfeit pretender to philosophy. In their day the itinerant "educators of men" had ceased to exist.

physical science and the new interest in the humanistic study of law and morals were fully represented in the Athens of Pericles. The old science, in its Eastern version, with its flat earth, had indeed been brought to Athens in that statesman's early childhood by Anaxagoras, and the tradition accepted by both Plato and Isocrates represents Anaxagoras as having been charged with the education of Pericles himself.[1] Anaxagoras had probably been compelled by the political opponents of Pericles to leave Athens to escape a sentence for "impiety" before Socrates was of full age,[2] but throughout the succeeding

---

[1] Isocrates (xv. 235) expressly says that "Pericles was the pupil of two sophists, Anaxagoras and Damon," and the same thing is implied by the well-known language of Plato in the *Phaedrus* (270 *a*) about the "elevation" which the oratory of Pericles owed to his association with Anaxagoras.

[2] The currently received chronology places the escape of Anaxagoras from Athens, where he had lived for thirty years, just before the outbreak of the Peloponnesian War, *c.* 432 B.C. But this is clearly inconsistent with the representations of Plato, who has given a long account of the hopes raised in the breast of the youthful Socrates by the Anaxagorean doctrine of Mind as the cause of the order in the Universe, and his subsequent disappointment. Plato insists on the point that Socrates only knew of the thought of Anaxagoras from reading his book (*Phaedo*, 97 *b* ff.), and clearly means that Anaxagoras had left Athens before Socrates was old enough to come into any personal contact with him.

years cosmologies of the Eastern type were still being taught there by his successor, Archelaus, and by Diogenes of Apollonia. The great geometer Hippocrates of Chios had established himself in the city. Plato assures us, and there is no reason to doubt the fact, that Parmenides and Zeno had visited the city, where Socrates made their acquaintance, while he was still a very young man, and Zeno must have lived there for some time, as more than one eminent Athenian paid him handsome fees for his instruction.[1] Plato's dia-

---

This fits in again with the statement that Anaxagoras had actually "educated" Pericles, and with the only natural interpretation of the Alexandrian chronological notice (D. L., ii. 7) that he "began to be a philosopher at Athens in the year of Callias at the age of twenty," and lived there thirty years. Since the chronologists placed his birth in 500 B.C., this will mean that he came to Athens in the year of Salamis (480 B.C.)—possibly as a conscript in the army of Xerxes—and left the city c. 450. (The archon's name Callias in our MSS. is presumably an error for Calliades, as the archon of the year of Salamis is called elsewhere.) These dates seem to be necessary, though my chronology has been called "impossible" by an eminent German authority. The current account appears to be based on the fourth-century historian Ephorus, with whom chronology was a weak point.

[1][Plat.] *Alcib. I.* 119 *a* mentions Pythodorus son of Isolochus and Callias son of Calliades as having each paid Zeno the high fee of 100 *minae*. Pythodorus, the person in whose house Plato makes Socrates meet Parmenides and Zeno, is a prominent Athenian commander of the

logues depict for us the sensation aroused by the
visits of the outstanding leaders of the "humanistic" movement, a Protagoras and a Georgias.
Protagoras, at any rate, must have had the *entrée*
to the circle of Pericles himself, who included him
in the Commission appointed to make a constitution for his important colony of Thurii (443 B.C.)
in South Italy, and Zeno seems also to have been
among his associates.

It seems quite certain that Socrates in early life
acquired a full knowledge of the science of the
age and a full mastery of its humanistic culture.
This is Plato's standing representation, and the
best evidence of its truth is that it is borne out by
the really remarkable admissions of Xenophon.
For his apologetic purpose he is anxious to prove
that Socrates took his own utilitarian view of
the sciences, that he thought one should know
enough of geometry to "take the measure of a
piece of land one is receiving or conveying," but
should not trouble one's head about "the intricate
diagrams," and enough of astronomy to be able
to "tell the time of night or month or year for
the purposes of a journey or voyage or night

Archidamian War, and Callias is the general who was
killed before Potidaea at the opening of the war in
431 B.C., when Socrates was himself in the Athenian
force.

watch," without concerning one's mind with "planets and wandering stars, and their distances from the earth, and their orbits and causes." Yet in both cases Xenophon at once adds, "yet he was not unfamiliar with the subject," "yet he was not uninstructed in these matters" (thus his alleged attitude was not the contempt of ignorance).[1]

Plato tells us more on the point in the autobiographical narrative which the *Phaedo* puts into the mouth of Socrates.[2] Socrates began, we are told, as an enthusiast for "research into Nature," eager to discover the "causes of the coming of things into being and their passing away." He studied the various current cosmological theories, Eastern and Western—it is indicated that he began with those of the two con-

[1] Xen., *Mem.*, IV. vii. 1–6. These concessions from Xenophon, which directly contradict his main thesis, can hardly mean less than that Socrates knew all that there was to be known about such subjects, though, as Xenophon says, he held that there are other things of which the knowledge is more indispensable.

[2] *Phaedo*, 96 *a*–100 *a*. This passage, along with the opening pages of the *Parmenides*, is our most important evidence for the way in which Plato conceived of the early mental history of his hero. Since the events fall roughly rather more than twenty years before Plato's own birth, the picture is, of course, an imaginative reconstruction, but there were plenty of members of Plato's own family circle from whom he could derive the necessary information

temporary teachers of the Eastern type of theory
at Athens, Archelaus and Diogenes of Apollonia—
and was particularly struck by the disagreement
about the shape of the earth. He knew the biological doctrines of the Sicilian Empedocles and
the theories of the Italian Alcmaeon of Crotona
about the brain as an organ of mental life, and
had been much troubled by mathematical difficulties connected with the notion of the *unit*, a
problem raised by Zeno. At first the flat contradictions between the tenets of rival theorists
brought him to desperation, but a passage read
to him from the book of Anaxagoras came as a
revelation. Mind, said Anaxagoras, is the cause of
all natural law and order, just as mind is the cause
of the orderliness and coherence of human action.
To Socrates this suggested that the universe at
large is the embodiment, like a properly con-
ducted human life, of coherent rational plan. If
Mind is the cause of the world's structure, the
earth and everything else in the universe must
have just the shape, position, place in the scheme,
which it is *best* that each of them should have.
He set himself to the study of Anaxagoras in the
hope that he had found a teacher who would put
an end to scientific uncertainty by showing how
it is *best* that every detail of the universe should
be disposed, and how it must therefore *be* dis-

posed in a world controlled by Mind. These hopes were speedily dashed when it appeared that Anaxagoras merely introduced Mind into his scheme to provide the initial impetus to the vortex-motion by which he supposed stellar systems to be generated, without making any use of the thought that a universe controlled by Mind must be the embodiment of intelligent plan. It was this early disappointment which led Socrates, as he humorously puts it, to conclude that he "had no head for the natural sciences," and to strike out a line of investigation and a method of his own.

The nature of this new method we shall have to consider later, when we are discussing the philosophy of Socrates. For the present, it is important to observe that the situation presupposed in the story told by Plato is historically exactly that which existed at Athens in the youth of Socrates, and that Plato is careful to direct attention to the fact by the copious details given of the conflicting doctrines between which Socrates hesitates. Plato is clearly not describing his own early history, since the intellectual situation had been entirely changed by his own time, and the theories he describes had become obsolete.[1] And

[1] Not to mention that by Plato's own account his own early ambitions seem to have been those of the man of affairs, not those of the student (*Ep.*, vii. 324 *b–c*).

we cannot well suppose that he means to describe the "growth of a philosopher's mind" in general (it is no essential of the process to be perplexed by the question of the shape of the earth). He clearly means to relate what he believes to be the facts about an intellectual crisis in the life of his hero Socrates; he had, as we have seen, ample opportunity for learning the relevant facts from Socrates himself and others, and we may therefore be reasonably satisfied that his narrative is substantially accurate. Of course, since he gives us no chronological indications except that the events belong to the early life of Socrates, it is quite possible that the intellectual revolution he describes in a page or two may have taken some considerable time for its completion.

Plato's statements ought pretty certainly to be taken in connection with the definite assertion made by Theophrastus,[1] the associate and successor of Aristotle, and the earliest writer on the history of Greek philosophy, that Socrates was actually a member of the school of Archelaus, the Athenian who succeeded Anaxagoras when that philosopher had to leave Athens. The statement passed from Theophrastus to the whole series of Alexandrian writers on the history of philosophy who took his work as their fountain-head, and can

[1] Theophrast., *Phys. Opin.*, fr. 4.

hardly be anything but true. Theophrastus himself was at least certainly in Athens in the lifetime of Plato, and may have been, as some accounts make him, an actual member of the Academy, and was a careful writer on such points of history. Moreover, his statement is confirmed by another associate of Aristotle, Aristoxenus of Tarentum, the writer on musical theory. Aristoxenus asserted[1] that the connection between Archelaus and Socrates began when the latter was a lad of seventeen, and continued for many years. He connected the statement with a good deal of scandal-mongering, the object of which is to discredit the memory of Socrates, but the worthlessness of his scandal is no reason for disbelieving his assertion about the fact of the association. Moreover, we also know that the fifth-century tragic poet Ion of Chios recorded the fact that Archelaus and Socrates visited the island of Samos together when Socrates was a young man.[2] Since Ion also recorded in his *Memoirs* his own meeting with Pericles and the tragic poet Sophocles in Chios in the year 441/40, it is a probable conjecture that the story about Archelaus and Socrates belongs to the same context, and that Ion met them together at the time of his

[1] Fr. 25 (*Frag. Hist. Graec.*, ii. 280).
[2] D. L., ii. 23.

meeting with Pericles. This was during the revolt
of Samos from the Athenians, and the Athenian
blockade of the island. Archelaus and Socrates
(then a man of twenty-eight or twenty-nine)
must be presumed to have been serving in the
Athenian blockading force, and the reason why
Plato makes no reference to the incident when he
has occasion to mention the campaigns of Socrates
will be simply that it was long before his own
time.[1] Plato tells us nothing of this connection of
Socrates with Archelaus, but it manifestly pro-
vides just the right framework for his story of the
introduction of Socrates to the book of Archelaus' old teacher.[2]

Apart from Plato's accounts of the meeting of
Socrates with Parmenides and Zeno, and his disappointment with the book of Anaxagoras, and
the just-quoted statements about his connection
with the school of Archelaus, we have no direct
information about the events of his life down to
the outbreak of the Archidamian War in the
year 431. We may, however, draw certain in-

[1] It follows that Socrates was serving against a force
commanded by the eminent Samian philosopher Melis-
sus.

[2] The book was presumably written in the author's
later years, after his final removal from Athens. Hence
its contents might come to Socrates as a novelty, in spite
of his association with Archelaus and his school.

ferences with fair confidence. It is natural to think
of him as for some time, at any rate, continuing
his connection with Archelaus and his associates;
we need not suppose that his engrossment in his
new method of inquiry was completed in a few
weeks or months. Perhaps we may even conjecture that when Archelaus retired—we do not
know when this was—Socrates was to all intents
and purposes his successor. This may sound
startling to us when we remember the vigour with
which the Socrates of Plato's *Apology* denies that
he has any "disciples," or has ever professed to
be any man's "teacher," but it is strictly consistent
with the denials of Plato. What Socrates is concerned to deny in the *Apology* is that he has ever
followed the profession of a paid "educator of
men," or taken "pupils."[1] This is quite compatible
with his having at some time before Plato's own
birth been the unpaid head of a body of "associates" over whose studies he had presided. (The
regular word for the relation of such a student
to the director of the group, we must remember,
was not *mathetes*, pupil, but *hetairos*, associate;
the difference lies in the implication of profes-
sionalism which is present in the former word, but

---

[1] *Apology*, 19 *d*, "should you have been told that I
undertake to educate men and charge a fee for it, that
is not true," is typical of the Platonic denials.

absent from the latter.) And there is in fact a good deal of evidence which implies that Socrates really had, in his earlier days, been something very much like the head of an organized "school."

This is clearly the presupposition of the caricature of Aristophanes in the *Clouds*. Socrates is burlesqued there as the head of a body of students —the burlesque naturally calls them "pupils"— who live together in his house, and it is taken for granted that they are supplied with such requisites of a scientific school as maps and apparatus. These inmates of the "notion-factory," as Aristophanes calls the house of Socrates, are depicted as combining two characters. They are a set of ragged and hungry ascetics with unusual "spiritualistic" views. This explains why a laugh is raised against them by calling them "wisest *spirits*,"[1] a phrase which in the Attic of the fifth century suggests *ghosts*. They are also devotees of astronomy, geography, and geology,[2] and profess a cosmological doctrine which we recognize at once as that of Diogenes of Apollonia, according to which everything consists of "air." This is why they are represented as praying to the Clouds, and why Socrates does his thinking swinging from a machine of some kind, to keep the air which con-

[1] Aristoph., *Clouds*, 94.
[2] Aristoph., *Clouds*, 184 ff.

stitutes his mind from contact with the damps of the earth's surface.[1] It is hard to see what point a burlesque of this kind could have unless there were a real basis of fact behind the distortion. Given the two facts, that Socrates held beliefs akin to those of the Orphics about the immortal soul, and that he was at one time of his life the leading spirit in a group of cosmological students with views of what we have called the Eastern type, Aristophanes' caricature has the requisite point; unless we grant this foundation in fact, it is silly.[2]

There is a particularly valuable section of Xenophon's *Memoirs*,[3] which must refer to a time in the earlier manhood of Socrates, from which we get some light on the reality behind the Aristophanic caricature. Antiphon the Sophist, says Xenophon, was anxious to detach the associates of Socrates, and apparently to attract them to himself. (We do not know the precise date of Antiphon, but it is certain that he is a figure of

---

[1] *Ib.*, 225 ff.

[2] So there might be wit and point in making Sir Oliver Lodge the hero of a similar burlesque; there would be no wit in giving such a part, say, to Mr. Chesterton. For a detailed study of the *Clouds* from this point of view, I may refer to the essay "The Phrontisterion" in my *Varia Socratica* (Oxford, Parker, 1911), pp. 129 ff.

[3] Xen., *Mem.*, 1. vi.

the days of the Archidamian War.) Accordingly,
he openly criticized Socrates unfavourably in the
hearing of these companions. He commented, in
the first place, on the ascetic life of Socrates, his
scanty raiment, shoeless feet, and meagre diet, all
characteristics made prominent by Plato and
Xenophon as well as by Aristophanes and his
brother comedians. He further criticized him for
his refusal to take a fee from his companions for
the services done to them. Services for which no
charge is made, he argued, may fairly be presumed
to be worth nothing. Socrates is made to meet
this second point first by drawing a comparison
between the "wit" who sells his knowledge and
the catamite who sells his "charms," and then by
explaining more precisely the nature of the relation between himself and the associates in question, with a view to showing that it is not of the
kind for which payment can be decently charged.
"A good friend," he says, "gives me the same
pleasure as a good horse, or dog, or game-cock
gives another man, or even more; if I know anything good, I teach it to my friends, and introduce
them to others from whom I conceive they will
profit in goodness. I join with my friends in un-
rolling the treasures of the wits of old times,
which they have left behind them in written
scrolls, and if we find a good thing there, we

pick it out, and think we have won great gain if
we become friends."[1] The Socrates depicted here
is quite unlike the man with the mission to all and
sundry so familiar to us from the personal recollections of Plato and Xenophon. He is quite definitely a student of "ancient wits," who must be
the early philosophers and men of science. He has
a circle of fellow-students round him, quite different from the leisured young men of wealthy
families who clustered round him in his later
years, as Plato says, for the pleasure of hearing
him expose the ignorance of public men[2]; and his
relation to this circle as director of their studies is
one which can plausibly be mistaken by Antiphon for that of a professional "master." Xenophon has here clearly preserved for us a valuable
notice derived from some Socratic man of a time
earlier than his own, and it is enough to prove
that the "notion-factory" of the *Clouds* is a distortion for comic effect of something real.

It is important to note that the fame of Socrates as a man of outstanding intellectual power
must have been established in this early half of his
life, and that, in particular, his relations with the
famous "sophists" must go back to this date. This
is plainly presupposed by Plato in more than one

[1] *Loc. cit.*, 14.
[2] Plato, *Apology*, 23 *c*.

place. The great encounter between Socrates and
Protagoras, the most eminent of the sophists, depicted in Plato's most dramatic dialogue, is manifestly imagined to take place before the outbreak
of the great war had become imminent. Alcibiades, who fought in the cavalry at Potidaea,[1] is,
in the *Protagoras*, still only on the threshold of
manhood; the eminent "wits," some of them from
cities which were to be "enemy states" in the war,
are all collected in the house of Callias on peaceful
and friendly terms. Now, in the dialogue it is
taken for granted that Socrates is already personally well known to all of them. He even
alludes,[2] as he does more than once elsewhere in
Plato, to having attended one of the less expensive
lectures of Prodicus. Protagoras, in particular,
has made his acquaintance some years before,
and pays him the compliment of saying that he
had then thought him the ablest man of his years
he had ever met, and has the highest confidence
in his future.[3] The relations of Socrates with these

[1] Plato, *Symp.*, 220 *d–e*.

[2] *Prot.*, 241 *a*. Cf. *Charm.*, 163 *d*, *Meno*, 96 *d*, *Crat.*,
384 *b*. The allusions would be pointless if they were
not to an actual fact.

[3] *Prot.*, 361 *e*. It is precisely because Socrates already
knows Protagoras so well that his young friend in the
dialogue comes to him for an introduction to the great
man.

men, as described by Plato, though the point is sometimes overlooked, belong to the early part of his life, before he had embarked on his "mission," and they are far from unfriendly. The "sophists" are never even mentioned by the *Apology* as one of the classes whom it became his vocation to expose. They admire his ability, though in a rather patronizing way, and his attitude to them is a characteristic mixture of respect for real attainments and polite amusement at their self-complacent unconsciousness of their limitations.

As Burnet has pointed out, we have besides more indirect evidence of the eminent position Socrates had won for himself before he was forty in intellectual circles far outside Athens. We know from Plato's *Phaedo*[1] the names of the persons who were present at his death-bed, and of one or two others whose presence was anticipated; and several of these names are confirmed, as those of friends of Socrates, by Xenophon. There were present, in particular, two young men from Thebes, Simmias and Cebes, once disciples of the Pythagorean Philolaus, and two Eleatics from Megara, Euclides and Terpsion. Simmias and Cebes are both named by Xenophon[2] among the men of real worth who frequented Socrates'

[1] 59 b–c.   [2] *Mem.*, i. ii. 48.

company with a single eye to the good of their souls. The accomplished "cosmopolitan" Aristippus of Cyrene, though not actually present, was on such terms with Socrates that Plato feels that some sort of explanation has to be given of his absence, and Aristippus also is made by Xenophon, who disliked him, to figure as a member of the Socratic circle and to receive a caustic rebuke from Socrates for his indolent and voluptuous life.[1] The special interest of the Pythagoreans in particular in Socrates is shown by the fact that the narrative of his death in Plato is given by Phaedo of Elis to the Pythagorean Echecrates of Phlius and a group of unnamed companions who are represented as enthusiastic admirers, eager for a full account of the great man's last moments. Now the native cities of most of these men, Thebes, Elis, Phlius, were "enemy states" during the Peloponnesian War, which went on, in spite of the "peace" nominally concluded in 421 B.C., almost continually from Socrates' fortieth year to his sixty-sixth. It seems to follow that his connection with the older men among these non-Attic

---

[1] *Mem.*, II. i. The animosity this chapter shows against Aristippus may be a real example of the influence of Antisthenes on Xenophon. It is as a rebuke to Aristippus that Socrates relates the apologue of the *Choice of Heracles*, which, according to Xenophon, he took from a discourse of Prodicus.

philosophers must have been originated before he was forty, and that the Pythagorean groups scattered up and down the Greek world must already in those days have looked up to him as a venerated teacher. Otherwise it is hard to understand why the young disciples of the Pythagoreans from Thebes should have been eager to resort to his company as soon as the conclusion of the great war made it possible. The same sort of "international reputation" is presupposed by a notice preserved to us from Aeschines that Aristippus of Cyrene in particular had first been attracted to Athens by "the fame of Socrates."[1] It is plainly implied in all these facts that Socrates, contrary to some modern representations, was from an early time in his life generally well known as an outstanding figure in intellectual circles far outside Athens. This is strictly in accord with Plato's account of the impression he made as a young man upon such eminent "foreigners" as Parmenides and Protagoras, but quite inconsistent with the quaint nineteenth-century theory which makes him into an eccentric "proletarian" of genius.

The same view of his position in early life is presupposed in the famous story, told at length by Plato in the *Apology*, of the declaration of the

[1] D. L., ii. 65.

Delphic oracle that "no man living was wiser than Socrates."[1] In spite of the scepticism of a few modern German writers, there can be no reasonable doubt that the delivery of the oracle is an historical fact. Plato could not have represented Socrates as telling the story at length before his judges, many of whom must have read the *Apology*, unless he had really talked about it; and it would have been insane to tell such a story, and to offer to produce witnesses to its truth, as Socrates does, unless the thing had really happened. Nor is there any difficulty in understanding why the Delphic priestess delivered the oracle, though some historians have puzzled themselves about the matter. As Socrates tells us in Plato, the oracle was given to his friend Chaerephon, who had put the leading question, "Is there any one alive wiser than Socrates?" Of course, as happens in such cases, Chaerephon was given the answer he had directly invited. The really instructive point is that the question should have been asked, for the putting of it means that Socrates must already have enjoyed such a reputation that an admirer could ask it without making himself ridiculous; it could only be asked about a man who was already famous in the circle round him as a "wit." Now, Plato makes it quite clear that,

[1] *Apology*, 21 *a* ff.

in his own belief, Chaerephon's question was put to the oracle before the outbreak of the Peloponnesian War, that is, before Socrates was forty. For Socrates is made in the *Apology* to account for his popularity with the young men of his later years as a consequence of the enjoyment they derived from his exercise of his mission to expose the ignorance of their elders, and to account for this mission as a duty laid upon him by the delivery of the oracle. Now this wide popularity with young men and growing lads is presupposed in Plato's dialogue *Charmides*, where Socrates, who has just returned from his campaign before Potidaea (431–430) at the opening of the war, is made at once to inquire after "the present condition of philosophy" at Athens, and the signs of interest in it on the part of "the young."[1] The delivery of the oracle, then, according to Plato, presumably belongs to a still earlier date.

It is important to dwell on this incident of the oracle, since, if Plato's representation can be trusted, it seems to have brought on a spiritual crisis in the life of Socrates. From the notices Plato has given us of his earlier life, we should naturally think of him chiefly as a prominent man in specially intellectual circles, at home in the advanced science of his age, though profoundly dis-

[1] *Charm.*, 153 *d*.

satisfied with the actual state of knowledge, and holding definitely original views of his own about the presuppositions and methods of philosophical inquiry. But as yet, though he is respected by all the intellectuals of his age, and has a group of devoted associates who look up to him as the foremost of all the "wits," there is nothing about him of the man with a mission to all and sundry to convince them of their ignorance of all that it most becomes a man to know, and of the supreme importance of "tending their own souls." That, according to Plato, was apparently just what distinguished the Socrates of later life from the Socrates of whom the pedant in Aristophanes' play is an intelligible caricature.

According to the version of the matter given in the *Apology*, the mission was the direct outcome of the oracle given by Apollo. Socrates explains that he was at first astounded by the god's opinion of him, since he was well aware that he possessed no particular wisdom. He therefore set to work to prove Apollo to be a liar by finding some one wiser than himself. He looked for such a man in the first instance among the prominent public men of the city, the "politicians," then among the poets, finally among the tradesmen and artisans, but in all cases to no purpose. In the first two classes he found no real knowledge at all;

neither politicians nor poets could give any intelligible account of the principles of their statesmanship or their art. The artisans had the advantage of the others in so far as they really understood their own trades, but, unfortunately, they fancied themselves to understand other and more important things equally well. In time, the true meaning of the oracle dawned on Socrates. The meaning was that mankind are universally ignorant of the one thing it is most imperative to know, how to conduct their lives aright, how to "tend" their own souls, and "make them as good as possible," and they are universally blind to this ignorance. Socrates is the one exception; if he, too, does not possess this supremely important knowledge, he knows its importance, and he knows his own ignorance of it; he is, at least, the "one-eyed" in a kingdom of the "blind," and the wisest of men, as men go. This is why he feels it a duty laid on him by God to persist in seeking the supreme knowledge, and to try to induce any man, fellow-citizen or stranger, who will listen to him to seek it with him. This, according to the *Apology*, is the way in which the "wit" Socrates became the "founder of moral philosophy."

It is, of course, plain on the face of it that there is an element of humour in the way in which the story of the oracle is used in this narrative, but, to have any point at all, it must be intended to be a record of historical fact in its main presupposition, that Socrates, in middle life, went through a period of crisis as a result of which he emerged a man with a clear consciousness of a "mission," and that the response of the oracle played a part in inducing the crisis. It may not be insignificant that Plato represents him as making the attempt to "convert" a young man of promise, Plato's own uncle Charmides, just after the campaign of Potidaea, during which he had experienced the twenty-four hours' "rapt" or "trance" described in the *Symposium*. If we knew more of the facts we might find that his "call" to be a prophet came to him during that vision, and Burnet may well have been happily inspired in suggesting that this explains why in Plato we find him so often using the language of military duty to describe his sense of the vocation thus laid upon him by God. At least it seems clear that by Plato's account the conviction of being a man set apart for a special duty to mankind dated with him from about the beginning of the Peloponnesian War, and not earlier. If we think of him as being what he must have been before Chaerephon had put his momentous question to Apollo, the picture drawn by Plato in the opening pages of the *Parmenides*, the account of his early days in the *Phaedo*, the

recollections of the unknown source from whom
Xenophon derived what he tells us about the relations between Socrates and Antiphon, and the
amusing burlesque of the *Clouds,* will be found to
harmonize with one another admirably.[1]

We can gather something from Plato and
others of the persons who must have formed the
"circle" of Socrates in these days before the great
war. In the first place, among his own most immediate friends, there would be his wealthy and
devoted friend and fellow-demesman Crito, a
man of about his own age. There was also the
excitable admirer Chaerephon, laughed at by the
comic poets for his sallow skin, dusky complexion, and half-starved appearance, and represented by Aristophanes as the confederate who

[1]This is just where I cannot entirely follow the admirable account given by C. Ritter in his *Sokrates.* He fully
recognizes that we have to accept Plato's account of
Socrates as well versed in all the "advanced science" of
his time, but suggests that this knowledge was deliberately acquired in early life as part of a deliberate preparation for the "mission." This seems to me out of keep-
ing with Plato's representation that the consciousness of
a mission only came to Socrates in mid-life. In any case,
we must not make the mistake of supposing that the
"divine sign" or "supernatural sign" had anything to do
with the matter. Plato makes no reference at all to the
"sign" in the part of the *Apology* which professes to
describe the origin of the mission; when he comes to
speak of the "sign," he treats it as something going back
to Socrates' childhood.

plays the "spirits" in Socrates' *séances*.[1] Some of
the older men who figure later on as "Socratics"
may probably be regarded as associates dating
from this general period, such as, in all probability, Aristippus of Cyrene and the contentious,
bitter-tongued, and ascetic Antisthenes; perhaps,
too, as we have said, Euclides and Terpsion, the
Eleatics of Megara. Plato, Xenophon, and
Aeschines were, of course, not yet born. Among
the eminent men who must have stood in relations of close personal intimacy with the philosopher from the very outbreak of the great war,
we have to remark first and foremost the most
brilliant of all, Alcibiades, the evil genius of the
Athenian democracy, which alternately spoiled
him and turned on him, and next, two kinsmen
of Plato's own, his uncle Charmides and his
mother's cousin Critias, both destined to disgrace
themselves even more deeply than Alcibiades.[2]

---

[1] Aristoph., *Birds*, 1553 ff., where Chaerephon's dusky
complexion is ridiculed by nicknaming him "the Bat."
At *Clouds*, 503, Socrates is made to promise old Strepsi-
ades that the reward of diligent study in his "school"
will be to "grow just like Chaerephon," which provokes
the startled reply, "Then, lack-a-mercy, I shall be a living corpse."

[2] The attachment of Alcibiades to Socrates is described
both by Plato, in the *Symposium*, and by Aeschines, in
the remains of his *Alcibiades*, as going back to the boyhood of Alcibiades, who must already have been a man

We may add to the list, on the evidence of the *Republic*, Plato's own elder brothers, Adimantus and Glaucon, and the family of the wealthy Syracusan manufacturer Cephalus, a *protégé* of Pericles, and father of the famous speech-writer Lysias. Plato and Aeschines further represent the philosopher as on familiar terms with members of the more immediate circle of Pericles, especially his morganatic wife, the famous Aspasia,[1] and the enormously rich Callias son of Hipponicus, the wealthiest Athenian of the day. Since Aeschines introduced into a lost Socratic dialogue, *Miltiades*, Miltiades son of Stesagoras, a member of the great house of the Philaidae, it would appear that Socrates had the *entrée* to the circle of Cimon as well as to that of Pericles. We further learn from Plato's *Laches* that he had an

---

of at least twenty when he fought in the cavalry at Potidaea. The *Charmides* describes the closer introduction of Socrates to Charmides, then a mere lad, just after the campaign at Potidaea, by Critias, whose connection with Socrates is presupposed as already existing.

[1] Socrates professes to be on familiar terms with Aspasia in Plato's *Menexenus*, and Aeschines wrote a dialogue on the subject of this friendship. Callias is the host who is entertaining Protagoras in Plato's dialogue, and also a leading figure in Xenophon's *Symposium*, the scene of which is laid in his house in the Piraeus in the year 421/20. He lived to a very great age, and the most prominent acts of his public career belong to the time after the death of Socrates.

old-established friendship with the families of
Thucydides son of Melesias and the great
Aristides; also that he was well known to the
wealthy, respectable, and unfortunate Nicias, the
leader of the more moderate and responsible section of the Athenian democracy in the years after
the death of Pericles, and the opponent of the
more militant party who made their idols succes-
sively of Cleon and Alcibiades. Plato several times
alludes to an early friendship with another prominent man of a still more remote time, Damon of
Oea, an eminent musician who was believed, like
Anaxagoras, to have "educated" Pericles, and to
have prompted some of his democratic measures.

The writers of the Alexandrian age also relate
anecdotes about a personal friendship between
Socrates and the tragic poet Euripides, a man
probably some twelve years his senior, and quote
in confirmation passages from contemporary
comedies in which Euripides was twitted with de-
riving the inspiration of his plays from Socrates.[1]

---

[1]For the Alexandrian gossip on the relations of Socrates and Euripides see D. L., ii. 18, 33. How little we
can trust some apparently confident assertions of this
kind is shown by the fact that in one such notice (D. L.,
ii. 44) Euripides is quoted as having reproached the
Athenians for the death of Socrates in his *Palamedes*.
Since the Palamedes is parodied by Aristophanes in the
Thesmophoriazusae (produced in 411 B.C.), the alleged

In the absence of any earlier and more precise information we cannot, of course, say whether there was any foundation for these jests beyond the spirit of inquiry and distrust of conventional opinion which is common to the tragedian and the philosopher. A famous younger tragic poet, Agathon, does appear in Plato as a friend and admirer of Socrates; the *Symposium* professes to describe a party held in his house to celebrate his tragic victory of the year 415 B.C. Aristophanes is one of the guests at the party, and Plato's assumption is that, in spite of his burlesque of eight years before, he and Socrates are on terms of perfect good-fellowship. Since, as we see from the *Apology*,[1] reminiscences of the *Clouds* were

---

allusion to the death of Socrates was written years before the event. Presumably the origin of the whole story is the simple fact that in Plato's *Apology* (41 *b*) Socrates refers to the story of the unjust condemnation of Palamedes as a parallel to his own case.

[1] *Apology*, 19 *c*. L. Robin, in his admirable *Introduction* to his edition of the *Symposium* (*Collection des Universités de France*), makes a most ingenious attempt to show that Plato's covert purpose in his treatment of Aristophanes in the dialogue is to avenge himself on the man whom he rightly regarded as responsible for the death of Socrates by pillorying him as *grand buveur et grand paillard*. This seems to me, speaking with all respect, a misunderstanding of one simple phrase, that in which the art of Aristophanes is said to be "wholly concerned with Dionysus and Aphrodite" (*Symp.*, 177

held by Plato to have helped to secure the condemnation of Socrates by creating a prejudice in
the minds of the judges, I cannot think it likely
that Plato should have imagined such a relation
for himself after the death of his Master. We
should rather accept his representation as historical fact, and draw the obvious conclusion that the
burlesque of the *Clouds* was well known at the
time to all parties to be meant simply in fun.[1]

From our knowledge of the size of the Athens
of Pericles and the manners of its inhabitants, we
may, of course, feel confident that any man who
was at all conspicuous in such a society, as Socrates manifestly was, would meet every one else
who was prominent. We cannot well doubt, for
example, that Socrates must have known such
men as Sophocles, Herodotus, Phidias, but it is
unprofitable to speculate on his relations with
such eminent contemporaries in the complete
absence of all definite information.

---

e). Dionysus is mentioned here as the patron of the
drama, and Aphrodite, I take it, in allusion to her association with the Graces, a compliment to the "charm"
which is so real a feature of Aristophanic poetry.

[1] Plato makes Socrates say as much in the *Apology* itself (18 *d*), where he clearly distinguishes the comic
poets themselves from other persons who repeated their
witticisms "out of spite and to misrepresent me."

III

THE LATER LIFE OF SOCRATES: HIS TRIAL AND DEATH

If our attempted reconstruction of the life of Socrates during the period of which we know least has been successful, we have to think of him down to the age of forty as one of the most outstanding "intellectuals" of a great age of mental and moral ferment, distinguished in the circles specially interested in things of the mind by a profound concern for the unseen moral order and a religious faith not common in the society around him in God and the immortal soul, as well as by a highly original view of the nature of the problems of philosophy and the methods by which they should be approached, and naturally thought of by the wider public as an amusing eccentric, a combination of pedant, paradox-monger, free-thinker, and necromancer, the character he wears in the *Clouds* of Aristophanes. We have to describe now the way in which his new-found activity as the preacher of a mission to all sorts and conditions of men, exercised during the years of a "world-war" which gradually hardened for Athens into a fight for bare existence, led to an increasing tension between the prophet and the mass of ordinary well-meaning citizens, and finally to his condemnation on what was really a charge of *incivisme*, disloyalty to the spirit of Athenian life. We must, of course, not forget that though the long struggle began as a war for the maintenance of a powerful empire, and though at the "Peace of Nicias" (421 B.C.), which suspended serious hostilities for two or three years, Athens, at any rate, emerged as still the most powerful of Hellenic cities, the later years of the contest, especially after the hopeless failure of the great Athenian adventure against Syracuse (in 413 B.C.), saw the imperial city fighting with her "back to the wall," and ended in the complete collapse of the old moral, political, and economic order. The well-meaning but short-sighted democrats who prosecuted Socrates were living in conditions very different from those of the secure and powerful, and therefore tolerant, democracy depicted in the Funeral Oration of Thucydides' Pericles.

Little is recorded of the external events of the life of Socrates during the first ten years of the

struggle, those of the "Archidamian War," beyond a few facts relating to his excellent military
record. But it must have been at this time of his
life that he married the only wife he is known
to have had, Xanthippe, since we know from
Plato that at the time of his death he left one son
who was a lad, *i.e.* not more than seventeen or
eighteen, and two small children, the youngest of
whom appears to have been an infant in arms.[1]
The names of Xanthippe and of her eldest and
youngest sons suggest good birth. The Alexandrian biographers represented Xanthippe as a
shrew with an ungovernable temper and a foul
tongue, but no hint of the kind is found in either
Plato or Xenophon. In the *Phaedo*, the only place
where Plato mentions her, she appears simply as
an affectionate wife with whom Socrates has a
prolonged last interview immediately before his
death, and Xenophon records nothing of her except that her eldest son thought her, as sons often
think a good mother, over-bearing,[2] and that
Antisthenes apparently did not like her.[3] Presum-

[1] The name of the eldest son, recorded by Xenophon,
was Lamprocles, those of the others, Sophroniscus and
Menexenus.

[2] *Mem.*, II. ii., where Socrates reproves his son for his
ungrateful attitude.

[3] *Symph.*, ii. 10. This dislike may account for the origin
of the later gossip.

ably, then, Socrates only contracted the marriage in mid-life. The Alexandrians had a story that he had also another wife, Myrto, said to be a relative of the great Aristides. But their stories about Myrto are contradictory. They make her sometimes the daughter, sometimes the granddaughter, of Aristides, sometimes the first wife of Socrates, sometimes the second. Sometimes they even assert that Socrates was married to both wives at once—apparently an invention of the scandal-monger Aristoxenus—and even tell a foolish tale that he took a second wife to comply with an imaginary Athenian statute providing for the repair of the loss of population due to the war by the legalization of bigamy.[1] (It would be chronologically possible that Socrates should have been twice married, but the silence of Plato and Xenophon makes it unlikely that he was.)

The military service of Socrates, so far as we are informed about it, belongs—apart from the probable early participation in the blockade of Samos under Pericles—to the Archidamian War. Plato relates that he distinguished himself by exceptional bravery at the siege of Potidaea (431–430 B.C.), and again on the disastrous field of Delium (424 B.C.), where the whole military

---

[1] For this worthless Alexandrian gossip see D. L., ii. 26, Athenaeus, xiii. 556 *d*.

force of Athens was routed by the Boeotians. A third campaign, before Amphipolis, mentioned by Plato[1] is commonly supposed to refer to the action outside that city in 422 B.C., in which both the Athenian and the Spartan commanders, Cleon and Brasidas, lost their lives, though Professor Burnet has suggested that the reference may be rather to the fighting which accompanied the foundation of Amphipolis, some fifteen years earlier. It is clear from Plato's accounts that Socrates' record for military courage and presence of mind stood very high. He is made to refer to his exemplary behaviour as a soldier with justifiable pride in the *Apology*,[2] and elsewhere Plato has put an encomium on his conduct both before Potidaea and at Delium into the mouth of a most competent eye-witness. In the *Symposium*,[3] after praising Socrates' endurance of all the hardships of the rigorous campaign, and relating the story of his remarkable "trance," Alcibiades records that in the fighting he was himself defended when wounded by Socrates, and says that the prize for valour—the equivalent of our V.C.— awarded to himself by the commanders, ought in justice to have gone to the older man. He adds that he was a witness of Socrates' presence of mind in the disastrous retirement after Delium,

[1] *Apology*, 28 e.   [2] *Loc. cit.*   [3] 219 e ff.

and that his self-command far surpassed that of his companion in the retreat, the general Laches. In the *Laches*,[1] Laches himself is made to tell the story, with the comment that if the rest of the Athenian force had behaved like Socrates, the defeat would have been turned into a victory.[2] Plato evidently means us to understand that Socrates was highly esteemed as a good soldier by the professional military men, and this, no doubt, helps to account for the regard felt for him at a later date by young men who aspired to a military career, like Xenophon and Xenophon's *bête noire*, the Thessalian *condottiere* Meno, after whom one of Plato's dialogues is named.

We have no record of any particular acts of Socrates between the retreat from Delium and the very last years of the renewed struggle, when Athens was making her final effort to avoid complete defeat. But we have to remember that it is just the years between the Peace of Nicias and the general renewal of war with the Spartan occupation of Decelea, a post in Athenian territory, in 413 which must have been most critical for

[1] 181 *b*.

[2] In D. L., ii. 26, Socrates is said to have saved the life of Xenophon at Delium, but since Xenophon was certainly an infant at the time, this must be merely an inaccurate version of the saving of Alcibiades at Potidaea.

his position. It was in these years that Alcibiades became the darling of the militant Athenian Imperialists, and inspired them with the fatal dream of the conquest of Syracuse which led directly to the undoing of Athens herself. The date of the party in the house of Agathon described in Plato's *Symposium* is laid early in 415, in the months just before the sailing of the great Athenian flotilla with Alcibiades as its principal commander; and Plato's picture of the commander "flown with insolence and wine" is, no doubt, meant also to recall the mood of general buoyant self-confidence in which the Athenian people were then indulging.[1] In a few months, the whole situation had changed. The great Armada had hardly been dispatched before Athens was convulsed by a gigantic "religious scandal." Alcibiades himself and many of his associates were accused of having repeatedly taken part in sacrilegious burlesques of the Eleusinian mysteries, an integral part of the religious worship of the State. Alcibiades was promptly recalled to stand his trial, made his escape on his way home, and was capitally condemned in his absence, along with his uncle

---

[1] We cannot, of course, say whether this "banquet" was a real historical event, though I should imagine it probably was. In any case, Plato has been careful to adapt the tone of his description to the state of feeling at the time.

Axiochus, also a member of the Socratic circle, and a large number of other distinguished men, apparently including several of those who figure in Plato's account of Agathon's banquet.[1]

Alcibiades made his way to Sparta and became at once the most formidable enemy of the democracy who had worshipped him. It was by his advice that, when the Spartans renewed hostilities, they took a step which changed the character of the whole war, the establishment of a permanent fortified post on Attic territory. Alcibiades was now openly a traitor as well as a man capitally condemned and religiously cursed for sacrilege, and Socrates must lie henceforth, in the minds of many worthy citizens, under the imputation of being responsible for the misdeeds of his supposed "pupil." It is true that after the failure of the anti-democratic *coup d'état* of the year 411—the so-called "oligarchy of the Four Hundred"—Alcibiades began to work for his fellow-citizens instead of against them, and was

---

[1]The fullest account—of course an *ex parte* one—of the whole scandal is that given by the orator Andocides —himself an incriminated party who had turned informer—in his speech *On the Mysteries*. It can hardly be a mere coincidence that three of the accused bear the same names as persons familiar to us from the *Symposium*, Phaedrus, Eryximachus (both speakers in the dialogue), and Acumenus, the father of the latter.

actually for a time recalled to Athens in triumph (407 B.C.), but the tide of popular favour soon turned, and he was once more in exile and general ill-repute when Socrates, for the first time in his life, suddenly emerged as an actor on the scene of public affairs.

This was in the autumn of the year 406 B.C. In the summer the Athenians had saved themselves at the eleventh hour from final defeat by a great naval victory off the islets of Arginusae, between Lesbos and the Asiatic mainland. But the victory had cost 25 vessels and the lives of 4000 men, many of whom, it was believed, might have been rescued but for the culpable negligence of the commanders. It was resolved to try the generals who had been in command for their lives, by the process known at Athens as *eisangelia*,[1] and the prosecution further demanded that the fate of all the eight commanders incriminated should be decided *en bloc* by a single vote. As this was a direct infringement of the normal constitutional procedure, the *prytanes*, the Committee of the Senate of Five Hundred whose business it was to prepare the *agenda* of the Assembly and preside in its meetings, to their honour protested

[1] This meant that the case was judged not by a sworn jury but by a vote of the citizen assembly. Thus it was analogous to a "Bill of Attainder."

strongly, and declared that they could put no such illegal proposal to the vote. Though the "sign" of Socrates refused to allow him to imperil his mission by mixing in politics, this had not prevented him from serving the city in its extremity by allowing himself to be nominated for the Senate, and he was, as it happened, a member of the Committee of *prytanes* on this occasion. After a long and heated discussion, the resistance of the other *prytanes* was overcome by the threat of the prosecutors to include their names in the indictment; Socrates remained unmoved, but his solitary protest was overborne. The generals were tried and condemned in a body, and the six of them who were actually in the hands of the authorities promptly executed; but Socrates was entitled to tell the story, as he did at his own trial, in proof of his sterling integrity and fearless devotion to the cause of law.[1]

---

[1] Plato's account of the matter will be found at *Apology*, 32 *b–c*; Xenophon tells the history of the trial at length in *Hellenica*, I. vii. Plato was probably, and Xenophon almost equally probably, an eyewitness of the proceedings. It is not quite clear from either narrative whether the scene in which all the other *prytanes* were intimidated into withdrawing their opposition took place in the Assembly itself or in the Senate. Referring to the event in the *Memorabilia* (I. i. 18), Xenophon says that Socrates was actually Chairman of the Committee of the *prytanes*. Nothing is said of this in his own

In the unhappy months of the year 404/3 which followed upon the capitulation of Athens to Lysander, Socrates had the opportunity to show that he was no more to be intimidated by an oligarchical *camarilla* than by a *canaille*. Athens had surrendered at discretion, and the brutal Spartan whom the fortune of war, or not improbably the treachery of her own commander, had made master of the situation had no notion of permitting the continuation of the democracy. Under pressure from Lysander a Commission of Thirty was appointed, with instructions to draw up a legislation for the future government of the city. Unfortunately, instead of performing the task assigned them, they constituted themselves a violently oligarchical revolutionary government, forced the more radical democrats to leave the city and establish themselves in the port of

---

much fuller narrative in the *Hellenica*, nor in Plato, and it is likely that he has made a slip of memory, as he certainly has, in the same sentence, in giving the number of the condemned generals as *nine*, whereas only eight were condemned, and only six actually put to death. The allusion in the *Gorgias* to an occasion where Socrates was Chairman of such a Committee and made some technical blunder in taking a vote (*Gorg.*, 474 *a*) seems to be to some much earlier event. It is certain that a man could be a member of the Athenian Senate more than once. For the details of this *cause célèbre* see Grote, *History of Greece*, c. lxiv.

Piraeus, and proceeded to disgrace themselves
by a great number of arbitrary executions and
confiscations of property, until they were forci-
bly expelled, and a modern democracy re-estab-
lished, in the course of the year 403. It was
Socrates' misfortune that two of his close associates were prominent in this disgraceful business
—Critias, cousin of Plato's mother, who was the
leader of the most violent party among the
"Thirty," and Charmides, her brother, who was
one of the principal agents. Again, as in the case
of Alcibiades, there was the appearance that
Socrates was "educating traitors."[1] He was not
himself, with all his respect for constituted authority, in sympathy with the kind of democracy
which had grown up after the death of Pericles,
and, unlike his old friend Chaerephon, felt no
call to leave Athens when the advanced democrats withdrew to the Piraeus. The temporary
masters of the city, however, knew well enough

[1] It is only fair to remember that these men probably
"lost their heads" under the temptation presented by
their situation. Critias had previously been known as a
poet and a man of wide culture whose political leanings
were decidedly democratic. If Xenophon is to be trusted
—though he was too young to be speaking on the point
from personal knowledge—it was Socrates himself who
first encouraged Charmides to conquer his natural bash-
fulness and take part in politics (*Mem.*, III. vii. 1).

that he was certain to criticize their procedure
in the same trenchant way in which he had been
accustomed to speak his mind about all public
affairs. They took occasion of his caustic comments on their first irregular executions[1] to cite
him before themselves and forbid him to converse
with younger men, on the pretext that he was
contravening one of their decrees which prohib-
ited the teaching of the art of speaking. Socrates
countered with some characteristically humorous
remarks about the impossibility of obeying such
an injunction, and was dismissed with a menace
by Critias.[2] It was a more serious act of intimida-
tion that the attempt was next made to implicate
Socrates himself in one of these administrative
murders.[3] He, with four others, received express
orders to arrest Leon of Salamis, a wealthy man
whose property it was intended to confiscate.
The others performed the task, and Leon was
duly murdered, but Socrates went straight home,
though he expected to pay for the disobedience

---

[1]He had observed that he had never before known a
herdsman plume himself on his skill in diminishing the
number of his cattle (Xen., *Mem.*, I. ii. 32).

[2]See the full story in Xenophon, *Mem.*, I. ii. 32–38.

[3]This, says Plato, was a common proceeding with the
"Thirty." They were anxious to protect themselves
against a day of reckoning by associating as many persons as possible in their criminality.

with his life, but for the counter-revolution which ended the Terror.[1]

It was the distrust aroused by Socrates' connection with "traitors" which caused the leaders of the restored democracy to bring him to trial in the year 400/399. Alcibiades and Critias were both dead, but the democrats did not feel safe while the man who was imagined to have inspired their treasons was still an influence in public life. Anytus, son of Anthemion, the instigator of the proceedings, seems to have had no unworthy motive, nor was he a political or religious fanatic. In politics he was a moderate democrat and a chief promoter of the amnesty between the conflicting factions after the downfall of the "Thirty," proving his loyalty to it by refusal to seek any compensation for grave personal losses under the usurpation. He was no religious fanatic, for in the year in which he supported the prosecution of Socrates for "impiety" he was also aiding the defence of the orator Andocides, then on trial on the same charge. Nor had he any desire to shed blood. The object of demanding the death sentence was merely to induce Socrates to consult his own safety by withdrawing into exile and letting the case go by default.[2] It has been

[1] Plato, *Apology*, 32 *c–d*.

[2] This is what is meant by the words of Anytus quoted at *Apology*, 29 *c*, that either Socrates should never have

asked why the prosecution was delayed until the fourth year after the restoration of the democracy. The explanation is that the revolution and counterrevolution of 404/3 had brought the ordinary work of the law-courts into confusion; the whole body of Attic law had to be revised and codified, and the Commission appointed for the work did not finish its task until the year 401/400. This is why the proceedings against Socrates could not be set on foot until 400[1]; in point of fact, Anytus made his move as soon as it was really practicable.

A prominent moderate politician like Anytus could not, of course, appear as the actual prosecutor in a case of this kind; this task was assigned to an obscure and comparatively youthful person called Meletus (probably not the poet of that name who is mentioned by Aristophanes in the *Frogs*, though he may have been this man's son). The prosecutor of Andocides for "impiety" was also called Meletus, and had been one of the party who executed the illegal arrest of Leon. What appears to be the speech delivered by Meletus against Andocides has been preserved for us in the collection ascribed to Lysias, and it is the

---

faced the Court or the death penalty should be insisted on.

[1]See the full explanation of the point in Burnet's note to Plato, *Euthyphro*, 4 *c* 4.

utterance of an extravagant religious fanatic. If, as is most probable, it was the same man who prosecuted Socrates, this will explain at once why "impiety" was selected as the formal charge. This would ensure that the tool of Anytus should do his work with a will. It is the worst feature in the conduct of Anytus that, to effect what he believed a salutary purpose, he should have used an instrument whom he must have despised. His own part in the proceedings was confined to the delivery of a formal speech in support of the prosecution. A similar part was played by a third speaker, Lycon, of whom nothing is known, except that Socrates in Plato's *Apology* speaks of him as a professional "orator."

As the offence with which it was resolved to charge Socrates was technically one against the State religion, the case fell under the cognizance of the official known at Athens as the *King*, the second of the nine annual magistrates called collectively the "archons," religion being specially his province. His business was, in the first instance, to see that the indictment was in proper legal form, to enter the reply of the accused to the charge, take the depositions of the witnesses on either side,[1] and make the other necessary

[1]Witnesses were neither examined nor cross-examined in court; the evidence consisted of written records of

preliminary arrangements for the bringing of the case before a popular jury. In the actual trial the *King* had further to preside over the proceedings, but it is important to remember that he had not the functions of a British judge. He could neither comment on the evidence nor rule out as irrelevant any matter introduced by either party. The jurors themselves were at once "judges of the law" and "judges of the fact," as well as judges on the question of what is relevant evidence. Since they were a numerous body—Socrates, as we shall see, appears to have been tried by a body of 500—only assigned to the case they were to decide by sortition at the opening of the proceedings, and voted by secret ballot, a trial before such a court was virtually one before a "public meeting," and this has to be borne in mind in reading Plato's account of the defence.

We do not, of course, know what the charge against Socrates as originally formulated by Meletus was, as the official record would preserve only the final version in which it was transmitted to the Court by the *King* for adjudication. In Plato's dialogue *Euthyphro*, the date of which is

---

what had been deposed in the preliminary stages, and no fresh matter could be introduced. Each party was, however, allowed to put questions to the antagonist, which had to be answered.

laid during the preliminary proceedings, Socrates is made to say that Meletus is prosecuting him as a "maker of novel gods,"[1] but nothing is said of this in the various accounts of the indictment preferred at the actual trial. The most accurate of these is probably that given in Diogenes Laertius,[2] which appears to be a transcript of the actual document as still preserved in the second century A.D. "Meletus, son of Meletus, of the deme of Pitthus, indicts Socrates, son of Sophroniscus, of the deme Alopece, on his oath, to the following effect. Socrates is guilty (1) of not worshipping the gods whom the State worships, but introducing new and unfamiliar religious practices; (2) and, further, of corrupting the young. The prosecutor demands the death penalty."[3]

---

[1] *Euthyphro*, 3 *b*. Presumably either the *King* declined to entertain the charge in this form, or Anytus induced Meletus to reduce it to the vaguer accusation of "novel religious rites."

[2] D. L., ii. 40. The authority alleged is Favorinus of Arles, a well-known scholar of the reign of Hadrian, who seems to have seen the original document. Plato and Xenophon agree with this as to the counts of the indictment, but Plato puts the charge of "corruption of the young" first, probably because it was the one treated more seriously by Socrates in his defence.

[3] The case was of a kind common in Attic procedure in which the prosecutor proposed one penalty, and the accused, if convicted, a milder one. The Court had to

We must be careful not to misunderstand either clause of the indictment. It is certain that the first charge does not mean that Socrates holds what we call "heretical opinions," nor yet that he disbelieves the stories of the conventional mythology, as he frequently confesses in Plato's dialogues that he disbelieves them. The religion of the Athenian State was wholly a matter of worship, or *cultus*; it had no theological dogmas and no sacred books. And it is certain that it was no offence against religion to disbelieve in the mythology of Homer and the poets; the current view of this was that the poets invented their stories for the entertainment of their public.[1] It is also clear that the charge of "novel religious

---

adopt one of the proposals, and was not allowed to take an intermediate line of its own. Presumably it was thought that, in such conditions, the culprit's own proposal would be a fairly reasonable one.

[1] Euripides made his Heracles denounce the whole mythology as an "unhappy fable of the minstrels" on the tragic stage itself (*H.F.*, 1346). Dr. Verrall's theory that the poet was running the risk of martyrdom by such declarations is quite unhistorical. Isocrates (xi. 38–40) makes an express point of attributing the misfortunes of the poets who related the stories (Homer, Stesichorus, Hesiod, Orpheus) to the righteous judgment of Heaven on their blasphemies. The person who first proposed to make false opinions in theology an offence against the State was Plato himself, in the tenth book of the *Laws*.

practices" has nothing to do with the "supernatural sign" of Socrates. From the point of view of the average Athenian, that would be only a case of the familiar fact of "possession," and it is also plain from Plato's *Apology*[1] that no reference was made to the matter at the trial until Socrates raised it himself. In fact, as Plato represents things, no one, not even the prosecutor himself, knew what this part of the accusation really meant. If we read between the lines, however, we may fairly discover in Plato's *Apology* both what was in the mind of Meletus and why he could not make himself more intelligible.

In Plato, Socrates deals with the charge in a curious way. He says nothing whatever to dis-

[1] At *Apology*, 31 c, where Socrates himself has occasion to tell the story about the "sign," he remarks that it is "presumably what Meletus has caricatured in his indictment." But the very fact that the tale has to be told by Socrates, is of course, proof that Meletus had not spoken of it. This is just why the "caricature" is said to have been made not in his speech but in the *indictment*. Socrates is humorously pretending, as Burnet says *in loc.*, that he has only just discovered what was meant by the mysterious language of the accusation. The fanatic Euthyphron in Plato (*Euthyphro*, 3 b) suggests that the "sign" may be what Meletus meant by calling Socrates a "maker of new gods," and Xenophon (who had, no doubt, read these dialogues) repeats the suggestion (*Mem.*, I. i. 3), but only to point out that there was nothing in the facts about the "sign" to sustain a charge of impiety.

prove the accusation of "introducing novel religious practices," and contrives to entrap Meletus into explaining that the phrase about not worshipping the gods of the State is meant as an imputation of sheer atheism. He can then, of course, point with triumph to the incompatibility of the two parts of the accusation.[1] It is easy to see that this is no more than a legitimate employment of humour to silence an accuser who either cannot, or dare not, explain his own real meaning. What his meaning was is indicated by an earlier section of the Platonic *Apology*,[2] in which Socrates maintains that, for want of anything more specific to allege against him, the prosecution is falling back on the stock accusations against "wits" and men of science as a class, and trusting to the caricature of himself as a man of that kind in Aristophanes' *Clouds* (now a quarter of a century old). The point is that the Ionian men of science had been accustomed to use the name "god" in a wholly non-religious way for "air," or whatever else they held to be the eternal substance of which things are made. This is why Aristophanes had made Socrates say that "the gods" were not "current coin" in his school, and had represented him as teaching that Zeus has been dethroned by "vortex-motion," and swear-

[1] *Apology*, 26 b–27 c.   [2] *Apology*, 18 a–19 d.

ing by a set of "deities of his own mintage,"
Chaos, Respiration, Aether, the Clouds.[1] Socrates
means, in fact, that the charge of "atheism" is
based on nothing more than an attempt to prejudice the Court by reminding it of the general
reputation of the old Ionian science. (Possibly,
also, though nothing is said which throws any
light on this in the *Apology*, Meletus may have
counted upon the recollection of the old scandal
of 415 about the "profanation of the mysteries,"
in which Alcibiades and other friends of Socrates
had been involved; and he may even have reck-
oned with the possibility that some of the jurors
would know that, in the more recent past,
Socrates had been in intercourse with young
Pythagorean admirers from cities which had only
just ceased to be "enemy states.") It now becomes
clear why the prosecutor could not explain himself more frankly. By the terms of the Amnesty
which had put an end to the confusion of the
year 404/3, no citizen could be called upon to
answer for offences committed before that date,
and no charge founded upon alleged acts committed at an earlier time could be entertained by
the Court. It would be the business of Anytus, as
a chief promoter of the Amnesty, to see that

[1]Cf. Aristoph., *Clouds*, 247, 252, 264, 367, 380, 627,
alib.

its conditions were not explicitly contravened.

The meaning of the second charge, "corruption of the young," is clearer. At the actual trial, indeed, the prosecutor and his supporters seem to have left their meaning vague. At least, Socrates is represented by Plato as professing to be much puzzled as to the particular kind of harm he is accused of doing to his younger associates. He says it can neither be teaching them the kind of "nonsense" about natural science which he is made to talk in the play of Aristophanes, nor exercising the calling of a professional sophist. It is notorious to every one that he has never been a professional "educator," nor had a "pupil," and no less notorious that the scientific speculations burlesqued by Aristophanes are not the subject of his conversations. If his prosecutors would be candid, they would have to confess that the alleged harm done to the young men who enjoy listening to his cross-examination of his fellow-citizens really means the exposure of the self-satisfied ignorance of their elders. Reading between the lines, one gathers that what really annoyed Anytus was that the criticisms of Socrates on the incompetence of politicians like himself tended to lower their reputation and to produce a critical attitude of mind towards the democracy and its institutions among the acuter of the younger generation—as was certainly the fact.[1] We might fairly infer that something worse than this must have been the real *gravamen* of the accusation, but that the prosecutors had reasons for not putting it into plain words.

What they chiefly meant we can still see if we turn to the *Memorabilia* of Xenophon, a defence of the memory of Socrates against a written attack by an "accuser," who is apparently the sophist Polycrates, an undistinguished writer who seems, a few years after the trial, to have worked up the case of Anytus and Meletus into literary form. Xenophon also mentions one or two minor ways in which the "accuser" misrepresented the character of Socrates. He charged him with teaching young men to make light of the respect due to the older generation, and with extracting an immoral sense from passages of the poets.[2] But

---

[1] *Apology*, 19 *d*–20 *c*, 23 *c*–*e*, 24 *c*–26 *b*.

[2] *Mem.*, I. ii. *passim*. The charges dealt with are teaching the young disrespect to their parents, criticizing such institutions of the democracy as the use of the lot in appointing to offices, educating Alcibiades and Critias, getting a bad sense out of lines from the poets. Since Socrates in Plato always treats the poets and their authority with irony, and since a good deal is made of this same charge in the *Apology of Socrates* by Libanius, the famous rhetorician of the fourth century A.D., which seems clearly based upon the pamphlet by Polycrates, it is likely that the point about the poets was urged at the

the particular "accusation" which Xenophon is most anxious to refute is something much more precise. The "accuser" charged Socrates with educating Critias and Alcibiades, and Xenophon argues at great length that both only associated with Socrates long enough to learn something of his unparalleled skill in speech, which they abused to their own ends.[1] Any reference to this alleged influence on the two great "traitors" at the trial itself was banned by the Amnesty of 404/3, and Anytus, no doubt, took care that the accusation should be left obscure. This is why we do not at once see the point of the reference when Socrates in Plato very pointedly denies that he has ever had an actual "pupil."[2] Polycrates, in his pam-

---

trial as part of the case, and it may well be that Socrates had really said some of the things alleged against him about the dubious morality of the poets.

[1] *Mem.*, I. ii. 12: "The accuser said that two persons who had been familiars of Socrates had done more injury to the State than any one; Critias was the most rapacious and violent figure of the oligarchy, and Alcibiades the most unprincipled and licentious of the democracy." Xenophon's reply is given at length, *loc. cit.*, 13–16, 24–28.

[2] *Apology*, 33 *a*: "I have never made any iniquitous concession to any of those who are said by a misrepresentation to be my disciples, or to any one else. I have never been the teacher of any man whatsoever," etc. The persons meant by "those who are said to be my disciples" are not Plato, and young men of his time.

phlet, blurted out what the forms of legal procedure would only allow Meletus to hint at. We see
from Isocrates that he charged Socrates in so
many words with being the teacher of Alcibiades.
Isocrates replies by denying the fact, exactly as
Plato makes Socrates himself do.[1] He must also
have said the same thing about Critias, and this
explains why fifty years later the orator Aeschines
could remind the Athenians that "you put Socrates to death because he had been the teacher of
Critias."[2] The motives for the prosecution are
unintelligible unless it is understood that Anytus
honestly held Socrates and his teaching responsible for the mischief done to Athens by the man
who had taught the enemy where to strike a
deadly blow at her, and the man who had been
the leader in the Terror which followed her
downfall. No doubt the distrust of Anytus was
provoked by the sort of unsparing criticism on

They had done no ill turns to the city for which any
one could think of making Socrates responsible. We
know from Plato himself (*Ep.*, vii. 325 *b*) that it was
only the condemnation of Socrates himself which led
Plato to give up the project of entering politics as an ad-
herent of the restored democracy.

[1] Isocrates, xi. 5: "You [Polycrates] gave him Alcibiades as a pupil, though no one had ever known of his
being educated by him."

[2] Aeschines, i. 173: "You put Socrates the sophist to
death, because he was shown to have educated Critias."

all the famous statesmen of the democracy of which Socrates often delivers himself in Plato's dialogues; almost certainly he had had his personal experiences of the humiliating effects of cross-examination by Socrates, but the real secret of his hostility lay deeper. Socrates had not, in fact, educated the two men who had done most to ruin their native city, but it was his misfortune that he had been a friend of both, and was inevitably supposed to have been something more.[1]

To the general surprise, Socrates did not go into voluntary exile, but remained quietly at Athens to await the trial, which came on in the spring or early summer of the year 399. No doubt, from his strictly constitutionalist point of view, the State had a right to hold an inquisition into the character of a citizen, and it was the citizen's simple duty to face the investigation. His defence has been preserved by Plato, who was present in court. The speech is so characteristic that we may be confident that Plato's version has reproduced it with close accuracy.[2] Socrates did not court

[1] We shall understand the situation better if we recall the obloquy heaped at the time of the recent War [1914–18] on a late philosophic statesman, mainly on account of an alleged sentence about his "spiritual home" which appears never to have been uttered.

[2] The doubts once raised on the point by certain scholars in Germany are really only due to their assump-

death; on the contrary, he said plainly that he
desired an honourable acquittal, provided only
that acquittal involved no compromise with the
truth.[1] On his relations with Alcibiades and
Critias he was careful, as loyalty to the spirit of
the Amnesty required him to be, to say nothing
beyond the one simple fact that he had never
been any man's "master." The popular miscon-
ceptions about himself he explained as due to
reminiscences of the burlesques of Aristophanes
and the other comic poets. As to the charge of
"novel religious practices" and "neglect to worship the gods," he was content to show that Meletus himself either would not, or could not, explain
what it meant. The allegation of being a "cor-
rupter of the young" he treated a little more
seriously, though still quite lightly, and offered to

tion that the first object of an accused man must always
be to "get off" at any price. That may be true of most
men, but it is not true of all, and least of all of a man
like Socrates.

[1] This is Plato's version (*Apology*, 19 *a*). Xenophon, in
his own later-written *Apology*, is puzzled, as some Ger-
mans have been, by the fact that the Platonic speech,
which he accepts as really reproducing the "lofty tone"
of Socrates, is not a judicious utterance for a man
merely anxious to be acquitted, and therefore puts forward the ludicrous suggestion that Socrates deliberately
provoked the Court to condemn him in order to "go
off" without suffering blindness and other infirmities of
old age! (Xen., *Apology*, 1–8.)

rebut it by calling the elder relatives of Plato and
other young companions in disproof of it. If his
object had been, as it was not, merely to secure
an acquittal on any terms, he should then have
gone on to say something about his excellent military record, and his courageous defiance of Critias
in the matter of Leon of Salamis, and there the
matter might have ended. But such a defence
would have been an act of treason to his mission.
Accordingly, he made no attempt to avoid the
odium always attaching in the suspicious Athenian democracy to the reputation of superior
"cleverness." He made the story of the oracle
which had declared him the wisest of men the
centre of his whole speech, and described without
concealment the way in which it had led him to
take up the work of convincing all and sundry,
from the leading statesmen downwards, of their
disgraceful ignorance of the one kind of knowledge which is of supreme moment, knowledge
how to make one's own soul and those of others
as good as possible. To desist from this mission,
he said, would be rebellion against God, and the
Court might rest assured that nothing short of
death would deter him from prosecuting it. Even
the military record and the affair of Leon were
brought into the speech merely to explain how
impossible dereliction of plain duty would be in

the speaker, and the story of the defiance of
Critias was joined to that of the equally bold
defiance of the democracy itself in the trial of
the Arginusae generals. It is not surprising, therefore, that the Court found a verdict of guilty,
though by a small majority. When we take into
account the tone of the speech and the fact that
the jury were, to all intents and purposes, a
public meeting, the result, so far, is creditable to
their liberality of mind rather than otherwise.[1]

Socrates had now to propose a penalty for himself as an alternative to that of death. Every one
must have supposed that he would propose banishment, and it is plain that if he had done so, the
Court would have been satisfied. But there again
he was true to his own principles. He held, he
said, that his mission had been a God-given bene-
fit to Athens, and that his deserts would properly
be recognized by conferring on him the exceptional privilege, given to victors at the Olympic
games, eminent generals, and a few others, of a
seat for life at the public table in the Prytaneum.

---

[1]We know from Plato (*Apology*, 36 a) that the majority for condemnation was 60. In D. L., ii. 41, it is
said that Socrates was condemned by 281 votes more
than those for acquittal. There must be some confusion
here. It seems most probable (see Burnet's note *in loc.*)
that the total number of the jury was 500, and that 280
voted for condemnation, 220 for acquittal.

Holding this view, he could not conscientiously propose to inflict punishment, or any other real evil, on himself. A mere fine, however, is no evil, so long as a man has the money to pay it, and Socrates was free in conscience to offer to pay such a fine. Accordingly, he offered to pay such a sum as he could immediately raise, 1 *mina*,[1] adding immediately that Crito, Plato, and other friends had prevailed on him to raise the offer to 30 *minae*, for which they were ready to give security. It is natural enough that the jurors should have been irritated by this uncompromising speech into voting the death penalty by a larger majority[2] than that which had found the verdict of *guilty*.

[1]To judge the adequacy of the offer, we have, of course, to take into account the high purchasing value of silver at the time. Apparently a *mina* was ordinarily thought a reasonable ransom for a prisoner of war. Thirty *minae* are frequently mentioned in the contemporary orators as a handsome dowry for a girl of middle-class family. We find Plato himself, a generation later, expecting to have to portion a niece with that sum (*Ep.*, xiii. 361 *e*). Xenophon (*Apology*, 23) makes a distinct point of denying that Socrates made, or allowed his friends to make, any such proposal. This is an intentional contradiction of Plato, and deserves no credit. Plato was present at the scene; Xenophon was absent in Asia, and apparently does not see that the offer to pay a fine is not a confession of guilt.

[2]According to D. L. (ii. 42), by 80 more votes than those given for the verdict. If this should be true, the

According to both Plato and Xenophon,
Socrates, at this stage, addressed a few final
words to the minority among the judges who
had pronounced throughout in his favour. Xenophon makes him do little more than repeat his
declaration of innocence, but Plato's version adds
something more characteristic. The sentence
which has been passed upon him, he says, is no
evil. At worst, death is no more than an un-
broken rest, and so no bad thing. But there is a
different belief, and it is made clear that it is his
own, that death for a good man is an entry on a
better life. In that case, Socrates may expect the
happiness of coming before the righteous and all-
wise judges of the dead, who will certainly reverse the decision of a misinformed and prej-
udiced Court, and of meeting with the famous
men of older days, including some who, like
himself, have been unjustly condemned by their
contemporaries; and there will be no danger there
that his vocation of cross-examining his company
will be cut short by another sentence of death.[1]

---

voting would be 360 to 140 (not, as Burnet says, by an
oversight on *Apology*, 38 *c*, 300 to 200).

[1] In Plato (*Apology*, 41 *b*) Palamedes is mentioned as
the typical example of the iniquitously condemned. It
would have conflicted with Xenophon's apologetic purpose to reproduce language in which Socrates professed
a belief so uncommon among Athenians at large as that

If this is the fate to which the Court is consigning him, they are unintentionally conferring the greatest of benefits on him.

The usual practice at Athens was that a condemned man was delivered at once to the "eleven" who had to administer the law, and that his execution followed within some twenty-four hours. The case of Socrates was an exception. There was a custom that a "sacred boat" should be despatched annually to the shrine of Apollo in Delos, in memory of the prehistoric deliverance by Theseus from the tribute of "seven lads and seven maidens" imposed by Minos of Cnossus. The city was religiously purified before the despatch of the boat, and the rules of ceremonial purity forbade any executions to be carried out until it had returned. It so happened that this

---

of the "life of the world to come." It is all the more significant that he has retained the reference to Palamedes (Xen., *Apology*, 26) as a parallel to himself. This is no first-hand evidence that Socrates spoke thus, since Xenophon was far away at the time, but it shows that he had read Plato's *Apology* and took it as a truthful narrative. His own version of the final speech is really Plato with the language about immortality suppressed. Similarly, at the end of the *Cyropaedia* (viii. 7, 17 ff.), where he has no apologetic purpose to consider, he puts into the mouth of the dying Cyrus a speech on immortality full of reminiscences of Plato's *Phaedo*. It is a fair inference that he, like Plato, had inherited the belief from their common Master.

period of ritual purity had begun in 399, the
day before the case of Socrates came on for trial,
and it was therefore necessary to decide what
must be done with him. (The matter could not
have been dealt with until the sentence had been
given, since no one, of course, expected that
Socrates, if convicted, would propose anything
but banishment for himself.) The wealthy Crito
did his best to induce the Court to allow Socrates
to remain at liberty until the return of the "sacred
boat," undertaking to give security that there
should be no attempt at escape,[1] but the offer was
rejected. Socrates was accordingly committed to
the prison of the "eleven," where he was kept in
chains of some kind, though not prevented from
enjoying the daily company of his friends. As
the boat was detained for a month[2] by contrary
winds, the whole of this period was spent in these
daily colloquies, and it appears that some of the
philosopher's foreign friends, such as Phaedo of
Elis and the young Thebans, Simmias and Cebes,
stayed permanently in Athens throughout this

[1]Plato, *Phaedo*, 115 *d*. Imprisonment was not a penalty
inflicted on citizens at Athens, except that debtors to
the Treasury were commonly confined until they had
paid their debt.

[2]That the delay was considerable is stated by Plato
(*Phaedo*, 58 *c*); the more specific "one month" comes
from Xenophon (*Men.*, IV. viii. 2).

time. Socrates also amused himself by taking to verse-making for the first time in his life. He composed a Paean to Apollo, and versified fables by Aesop.[1] He accounted for this by saying that all through life he had been haunted by a dream in which he was commanded to "practise music." In the past he had supposed that the meaning of the injunction was that he should labour on his "mission," since "philosophy is the truest music." Since the dream was repeated during his imprisonment, when the mission could no longer be exercised, piety bade him to comply with its directions in their literal sense.

Socrates' friends made a final attempt to save him by corrupting his guardians to connive at escape. All the preparations had been made, and, to obviate any reluctance the philosopher might feel to implicate fellow-citizens in an affair which might have unpleasant consequences for them, Theban admirers, on whom the Attic authorities could have no hold, were prepared to provide all the necessary funds.[2] Socrates, true to his character, refused to avail himself of the opportunity, and the reason for his refusal is explained in Plato's *Crito*. It is that escape would stultify

[1] Plato, *Phaedo*, 60 *d* ff. The alleged opening lines of both compositions are given by D. L. (ii. 42).

[2] *Crito*, 45 *b*.

the professed principles of a lifetime. The verdict
of the Court which had sentenced him to death
was false in fact, and had been procured by mis-
representations discreditable to the prosecutors.
But it was the legal finding of a legitimately constituted Court, and the State had therefore a
right to its enforcement. The wrong committed
against Socrates had been committed not by
Athens, but by Anytus and Meletus; if Socrates
should break prison, this would be a crime against
the State and its laws themselves, an act of treason against the spirit of citizenship. Socrates had
all the loyalty to conscience of a modern "con-
scientious objector," combined with a respect
for the "public conscience" which is, unfortunately, unusual in such quarters.

The story of his last day on earth, as related in
the *Phaedo* by Plato, who, though not himself
present, had the fullest means of getting information from those who were, and was writing to
be read by them, is perhaps the greatest thing in
the prose literature of Europe. Socrates, who had
been warned of the exact day of his departure
two days earlier "in a dream," was found by his
friends in company with his wife and her child,
whom he sent home at once, apparently for
necessary rest. (Xanthippe and the baby seem to
have been spending the night in the prison.) He

bore himself with his usual gay constancy—"merriment" was as native to him as to Thomas More —and spoke much of his conviction that death, to a good man, is the rise of the curtain on a drama for which his whole life has been a rehearsal—the drama of the soul's liberation from confinement in the "pound" or "pen" of the body, where it has hitherto been confined by God, for His own good purposes, into the greater freedom of a better world, where truth and reality will be known face to face, and no longer "peeped" at "through lattices of eyes." A life spent in "philosophy"—the pursuit of truth for its own sake—is itself one long preparation for this blissful enlargement, as it is also the true service of God, who requires us simply to "make the soul"—that within us which thinks and knows —"as good as possible." Since he had spent his own life in this service of God, he said, he could look forward with confidence to the future awaiting him. Finding that his young friends from Thebes, Cebes and Simmias, were much troubled with "scientific" doubts that the soul may be no more than a perishable function of the body, he devoted his last morning to reasoning with them in his own justification, on the "real distinction of the soul from the body," and the grounds for believing that it is neither born with the body nor dies with it, but shares in the eternity of the Truth and Goodness which it knows. Through the whole discussion he showed himself free alike from depression by the prospect of imminent death, and from over-anxiety to cling to a comforting belief without giving full weight to all there might be to urge against it.

The argument finished—it ended with an imaginative picture of the doom of the good and the wicked in the unseen world—Socrates retired to prepare his own body for its funeral, that the necessary offices might not have to be done by others upon his corpse, and to hold a last private interview with the "children and women of his family." It must have been a long interview, for the darkness was already closing in on the spring or summer day when he returned to his friends. At sunset the "officer of the eleven"—as we should say, "the governor of the prison"—took a formal farewell, not without tears, of the "bravest, gentlest, best" man who had ever been committed to him. Then appeared the actual minister of death, bearing the draught of poison[1] by which

[1]Plato never mentions the name of the poison employed, but we know from accounts of other executions that hemlock was commonly used. The description of the death of Socrates shows that the drug acted by a refrigeration, spreading upwards from the feet, and that death, accompanied by a spasm, ensued when the heart

the condemned were executed at Athens. Socrates took the bowl with composure, and would have made a "libation," as a grace before drinking, but for the warning that the quantity of the potion prepared would admit of no waste. With a few words of prayer for a "happy passing," he drained the cup without any sign of repugnance. At this point the composure of the company of friends broke down; several of them were openly weeping, and one, Apollodorus, was so hysterical that he had to be recalled to decorum by Socrates himself. On the instructions of the prison official Socrates walked about the room for a time, until his feet began to feel heavy; then he lay down on his pallet and covered his head. Manual exploration showed that a numbness was gradually advancing upwards towards the region of the heart. After an interval of silence the old man uncovered his head for a moment with the request, "Crito, we owe a cock to Asclepius; do not forget to pay the debt." These were his last words. Was he recollecting dimly some incident, connected perhaps with an infantile illness in his family? Or did he promise the gift to the god of healing because he hoped to wake from the fever of life

---

was affected. For a medical opinion to the effect that the agent used in this case was hemlock, see Burnet, *Phaedo*, Appendix I.

cured? A little later there was a convulsive movement; the body was uncovered and life found to be gone. "Hereupon Crito closed his eyes and mouth, and so ended our friend, the man we hold best, wisest, most upright of his age."

The Alexandrians told stories of the remorse which fell upon the Athenians, how they put Meletus to death and honoured Socrates with a statue. But these tales have long been recognized to be fabulous. Socrates was feared by certain prominent politicians of the restored democracy as the supposed instigator of Alcibiades and Critias, and these politicians desired to get him out of Athens. But there was no wish to take his life, and he can never have been the mark of general hostility. Nearly forty-five per cent. of his judges, as we have seen, were for acquitting him. And there was no general revulsion of feeling after his death; public sentiment remained divided about Socrates, as about Alcibiades himself. This is shown by the language used by Isocrates, who had known him, though not as an intimate. Isocrates tells Polycrates that when he charged Socrates in his pamphlet with having been the preceptor of Alcibiades he was saying what was not true, but had it been true, would have been a still greater compliment to the memory of Socrates than any paid it by "those who are accustomed to eulogize him."[1] Socrates owes his immortality of fame as the martyr of philosophy not to any melodramatic outburst of popular sentiment on the part of an emotional democracy, but to the Providence which gave him as younger friend and follower the one man in history who has combined supreme greatness as a philosophic thinker with equal greatness as a master of language, and so has been, directly or indirectly, the teacher of all thinking men since his own day.

[1]Isocrates, xi. 5–6. Isocrates had, no doubt, read Plato's *Apology*, but his language implies that he counted on a party among his readers who cherished the memory of Socrates. For the division of opinion about Alcibiades compare Isocrates, xvi, on the one side with Lysias, xiv, on the other.

IV

THE THOUGHT OF SOCRATES

What is the real significance of Socrates in the history of European thought? We may at once dismiss two views which have sometimes been held on this question as incapable of explaining the facts which need to be accounted for. Socrates was not a mere preacher of a commonplace morality of acting like an *homme de bien* for the utilitarian reason that bad ways "do not pay"—a view of him suggested by undue attention to certain parts of Xenophon's *Memorabilia*. Such a man would hardly have been put to death as a public danger; he would not have won the devotion of Plato, nor the general admiration of all the outstanding men of his age, or been caricatured as he was actually caricatured by Aristophanes. You may say Anytus misunderstood his man, Plato "idealized" him, Aristophanes distorted his features. But there must have been something to prompt the misunderstanding, the idealization, the distortion. The subject of them must have been in some way an extraordinary, in fact a *singular* character, an "original," and we have to discover in what his singularity consisted. Nor can Socrates have been what he has sometimes been taken to be by superficial readers of Plato, a mere sceptic, quick at disturbing the convictions of others by ingenious questions, but without convictions, and intense convictions, of his own. Mere clever scepticism is as ephemeral in its results as it is temporarily dazzling; Socrates created the intellectual and moral tradition by which Europe has ever since lived. *How* this could be is what has to be explained.

At bottom the answer seems to be a very simple one, and it may be best be given in the elementary way in which it has been stated by Burnet.[1] It was Socrates who, so far as can be seen, created the conception of the *soul* which has ever since dominated European thinking. For more than two thousand years it has been the standing assumption of the civilized European man that he has a *soul*, something which is the seat of his normal waking intelligence and moral character,

[1] See, in particular, Burnet's essay, "The Socratic Conception of the Soul" (*Proceedings of the British Academy*, viii. 235–260), and his article, "Socrates," in Hastings' *Encyclopaedia of Religion and Ethics*, xi.

and that, since this *soul* is either identical with himself or at any rate the most important thing about him, his supreme business in life is to make the most of it and do the best for it. There are, of course, a minority of persons who reject this theory of life, and some of them even deny the existence of a soul, but they are a small minority; to the vast mass of Europeans, to this day, the existence and the importance of the soul is a doctrine so familiar that it seems self-evident. The direct influence, indeed, which has done most to make the doctrine so familiar to ourselves is that of Christianity—but when Christianity came to the Graeco-Roman world it found the general conception of the soul which it needed already prepared for it by philosophy. Now the remarkable thing is that we find this conception of the soul as the seat of normal intelligence and character current in the literature of the generation immediately subsequent to the death of Socrates; it is common ground to Isocrates, Plato, and Xenophon, and thus cannot be the discovery of any one of them. But it is wholly, or all but wholly, absent from the literature of earlier times. It must thus have originated with some contemporary of Socrates, and we know of no contemporary thinker to whom it can be attributed other than Socrates himself, who is consistently

made to teach it in the pages of both Plato and
Xenophon.

Of course, we hear frequently enough in Greek
literature, from Homer onward, of a thing which
is called the *psyche*. But the important point is
that there is perhaps no single passage in the
earlier literature in which *psyche* means what
soul has meant to us for so many centuries, the
conscious personality which may be wise or
foolish, virtuous or vicious, according to the
"tendance" and discipline it gets. In the earlier
literature *psyche* regularly means one of two
things, neither identical with what we have been
taught to call the *soul*, according as the word is
being used with associations derived from Homer
or from Orphic religion.

In Homer the *psyche* means quite literally the
ghost. It is something which is present in a man
so long as he lives, and leaves him at death. It
is, in fact, the "ghost" which the dying man
"gives up." But it is not the *self;* for Homer the
"hero himself," as distinguished from his *psyche*,
is his *body*. Though a man cannot live when his
psyche has left him, the *psyche* is never thought
of as having anything to do with the "mental
life," as we now call it; that is carried on, in
Homer's language, by the *kear*, heart, or the
phrenes, midriff, both bodily organs. And the

psyche which has left the body has no consciousness whatsoever, any more than a man's shadow or his reflection in a pool; all that the departed *psyche* can do is to be seen from time to time in the dreams of the living. It is thus, at bottom, no more than the "breath" which a man draws while he is alive and exhales finally when he "expires." Ionic science, in its account of the *psyche*, starts from these conceptions and carries the de-individualization of *psyche* still further. Its reigning view is that my *psyche* is simply that part of the ambient "air" which I inhale. "Air" is itself a "god," and so is conscious, and that is why I am conscious just so long as I can continue to replenish my system with fresh portions of "the god." When I "breathe my last," the divine air in me simply goes back again to mingle with the common stock of the "air" in the world at large; there is no real and permanent individual bearer of my "personality." (In the philosophy of Heraclitus, indeed, we can see that the "soul"— which he supposed to be not "air" but "fire"— was very important, but it is a standing contradiction in this thinking that it at once has got to possess some sort of permanent individuality, in order to pass through the vicissitudes of birth, death, and re-birth, and yet is only a temporarily detached portion of the cosmic "fire.")

In the Orphic religion, on the other hand, as in the kindred religion of the early Pythagoreans, the *psyche* is a more important thing. It has a permanent individuality, and is consequently immortal, and, in fact, a temporarily "fallen" and exiled divinity. The great concern of the devotee is to practise rules of life, partly moral, partly ceremonial, which will lead to the final deliverance of the *psyche* from the "wheel of birth," and its restoration to its place among the gods. But it is not the *soul*, if by the *soul* we mean "that within us"—to use the words of Socrates in Plato —"in virtue of which we are pronounced wise or foolish, good or bad." It is supposed by the Orphics to manifest its activity just when what we should call the "normal" waking self is in abeyance—in dreams, visions, trances. As Pindar puts it, "[the psyche] sleeps while the members are active, but in men's sleep it bodes forth in many a dream the impending issues of weal and woe."[1] *My* intelligence and *my* character thus do not belong to the *psyche* in me, and its immortality, important as it is held by the Orphic to be, is not, properly speaking, *my* immortality. Where the *psyche* is spoken of, exceptionally, in earlier literature as the source of any actions in the everyday waking life, it is commonly mentioned

[1] Fr. 131, Bergk.

in connection with the freakish appetites of which sober sense disapproves.[1] It seems certain that at Athens in the fifth century the word *psyche* suggested to the ordinary man no more than "ghost" does to us, and this is why Aristophanes in the *Clouds* talks about Socrates and his companions as σοφαὶ ψυχαί—he means to suggest that the life of these "thinkers" is no better than that of so many "ghosts." So φιλοψυχία, concern for one's *psyche*, meant the cowardly hanging on to "dear life" which leads a man to "funk" in the field.

Clearly, what is needed for the development of a "spiritual" morality and religion is that the Orphic insistence on the supreme importance of "concern for the interests of the *psyche*" shall be combined with the identification of this supremely precious *psyche* with the seat of normal personal intelligence and character. This is just the step which is taken in the doctrine of the soul taught by Socrates in both Plato and Xenophon, and it is by this breach with the Orphic tradition as much as by giving the conduct of life the central place which earlier thinkers had given to

[1] As when the Cyclops in Euripides says he will for once "do his *psyche* a good turn" by a cannibal debauch (*Cycl.*, 340). So the Romans said *genio indulgere* in the same sense, and *anima causa agere*, "to act on one's whim."

astronomy or biology that Socrates, in the hackneyed Ciceronian phrase, "brought philosophy down from heaven to earth." In other words, what he did was definitely to create philosophy as something distinct at once from natural science and from theosophy, or any amalgam of the two, and to effect this result once for all. The soul, as he conceives of it, has all the importance and the permanent individuality of the Orphic *psyche*. For reasons already given, it seems plain to me that we must believe Plato's representations about his Master's firm conviction of the soul's immortality, and in the mouth of a Greek this means its essential *divinity*. This is the real justification of a mission to preach to all men, in season and out of season, the single duty of "tending the soul," and "making it as good as possible," whatever the cost to one's fortunes or one's body. But the identification of the soul which it is our first duty to "tend" with the normal self means, of course, that the "tendance" will not consist in the practice of ritual abstentions and purifications, but in the cultivation of rational thinking and rational conduct. A man's duty will be to be able to "give account" of, to have a rational justification for, what he believes and what he does. It is precisely by asserting and doing that for which we can give no rational justification that we display our

indifference to the duty of "tending" our souls.
This is why when Socrates came to discharge
his mission his first task was to convict the un-
enlightened of "ignorance," to show them how
little intelligent justification they have for what
they do or believe.

This Socratic doctrine of the soul, we must
note, is neither psychology, in our sense of the
word, nor psycho-physics. It tells us nothing on
the question what the soul *is*, except that it is
"that in us, whatever it is, in virtue of which we
are denominated wise and foolish, good and evil,"
and that it cannot be seen or apprehended by any
of the senses. It is no doctrine of the "faculties"
of the soul, any more than of its "substance."
The thought is that the "work" or "function"
of this divine constituent in man is just to *know*,
to apprehend things as they really are, and consequently, in particular, to *know* good and evil,
and to *direct* or *govern* a man's acts so that they
lead to a life in which evil is avoided and good
achieved. What Socrates is concerned with is thus
neither speculative nor empirical psychology,[1]

[1] Empirical psychology, founded by Alcmaeon of Crotona, is represented, in the age of Socrates, by those
scientific Pythagoreans who taught that the soul is the
"attunement of" the melody given out by the body, a
doctrine, as is shown in the *Phaedo*, quite inconsistent
with the *religion* of both Pythagoras and Socrates.

but a common principle of epistemology and ethics. To "make the soul as good as possible" would be on the one side to attain the knowledge of existence as it really is, on the other to base one's moral conduct on a true knowledge of "moral values." In both spheres the one thing to be overcome is the putting of "opinion," "fancy" (*doxa*), assumptions which cannot be justified as true, in the place of knowledge. As science is ruined by the confusion of fancy with fact, so practical life is spoiled by a false estimate of good. We have now to see how this conception of knowledge of the truth as the one supreme business of the soul, and therefore of man, works out into the beginnings of a theory both of science and of moral conduct. We might be confident, even without the plain indications of Plato to guide us, that Socrates' interest in the scientific problem belongs more particularly to the earlier part of his life, and that the ethical side of his thinking must have been almost exclusively dominant in the later years devoted to his mission to mankind. But we shall take the two things in the reverse order, in view of the much more general consensus of scholars on the characteristic features of the Socratic ethic.

1. *Ethics.*—When Aristotle has occasion to speak of the distinctive moral teaching of Soc-

rates, he ascribes to him three special tenets, all at first sight paradoxical: (*a*) virtue, *moral* excellence, is identical with knowledge, and for that reason, *all* the commonly discriminated virtues are one thing; (*b*) vice, bad moral conduct, is therefore in all cases ignorance, intellectual error; (*c*) wrong-doing is therefore always involuntary, and there is really no such state of soul as that which Aristotle himself calls "moral weakness" (*acrasia*), "knowing the good and yet doing the evil." Aristotle pretty clearly took these statements directly from his reading of one particular great dialogue of Plato, the *Protagoras*, where they are all to be found, but they fairly describe the substance of what Socrates has to say about morality in the dialogues of Plato's earlier period, and they all reappear in a more commonplace form in the *Memorabilia* of Xenophon. We shall have the key to them if we can discover the point of view from which they cease to be paradoxes and begin to appear obvious.

We may most conveniently start with what appears to be the most violent paradox of all, the assertion that all wrong-doing is involuntary. "Moral weakness," the fact that men do what they themselves confess to be wrong, and that they do so without any forcing, is one of the most familiar facts of experience, and we are not to suppose that Socrates means to deny this. He means to say that the popular phrase we have just used gives an inadequate analysis of the fact. A man often enough does evil *in spite of* the fact that it is evil; no man ever does evil simply *because* he sees it to be evil, as a man may do good simply because he sees it to be good. A man has temporarily to sophisticate himself into regarding evil as good before he will choose to do it. As it is put in the *Gorgias*, there is one fundamental desire which is ineradicable in all of us: the desire for *good* or *happiness*. It is possible, in the case of all other objects, to prefer the appearance to the reality, the outward show, *e.g.* of power, or wealth, to the thing itself, but no one can wish for the show of good or happiness rather than the reality: this is the one case where the shadow cannot possibly be esteemed above the substance. To say that vice is involuntary means, therefore, that it never brings the vicious man that on which his heart, whether he knows it or not, like the heart of every one else, is really set. The typical Greek "monster of wickedness," the "tyrant" who has raised himself above all the laws, may spend his whole life "doing as he pleases" with the persons and property of all men, but just because he *always* does "just as he pleases," he never gets what he really wishes for. He wishes for felicity, and gets the extreme of infelicity, a hopelessly diseased *soul*. It would be better to be a criminal under sentence of death, because death may be just the sharp "surgery" needed to cure the malady of the criminal's soul. Thus, if a man really knew as assured and certain truth, of which he can no more doubt than he can doubt of his own existence, that the so-called "goods" of body and "estate" are as nothing in comparison with the good of the soul, and knew what the good of the soul is, nothing would ever tempt him to do evil. Evil-doing always rests upon a false estimate of goods. A man does the evil deed because he falsely expects to gain good by it, to get wealth, or power, or enjoyment, and does not reckon with the fact that the guilt of soul contracted immeasurably outweighs these supposed gains. Socrates thus agrees on one point with Hedonism, that wrong-doing is due to miscalculation; but the miscalculation is not one of "amounts of pleasure," but of values of good.[1]

[1]This is the real point of the argument in Plato's *Protagoras*, where Socrates appears at first sight to be talking Hedonism. He wants to prove to the "many" that, *even on their own theory* that good and pleasure are the same thing, it is not a paradox to identify the courage of the virtuous man with knowledge, since they will admit that the coward who runs away from danger is making a false computation of the "balance of pleasures and pains."

We see now what is meant by saying that all the virtues are one thing, and that thing knowledge. The current view of mankind, in Socrates' day as in ours, was that the moral virtues are a plurality; each is quite unlike the others, and you can have one in the highest degree without having any vestige of another—can, for example, be the *brave des braves* and yet as profligate as brave, or the most continent of men and yet the most grasping and unfair. Now Socrates admits that this is true, if by the virtues you mean what he calls in Plato "vulgar virtue," the sort of outward respect paid to an accepted code of conduct by men who have no personal conviction of the supreme importance of the soul, and the identity of true happiness with its "health," and merely conduct themselves decently because the habits of their society require it of them, and they expect to be made uncomfortable if they behave otherwise. But this "vulgar" virtue is a mere illusory counterfeit of the true. True virtue is an affair of intense conviction, personal *knowledge* of the true moral "values." There is thus one single principle behind all its various manifestations in the varied situations of life. A man who has grasped this principle with the assured insight of knowledge cannot, then, apply it in some situations and not in others. Real knowledge of what is good for the soul will display itself in a right attitude to all the situations of life, and thus in the "philosopher's" life the apparent dividing lines between one type of moral excellence and another will vanish. The whole of his conduct will be the exhibition of one excellence, steady and assured certainty of the true "scale of good." This explains the curious fact that more than one of the Platonic dialogues ends in a singular, apparently negative result. We are invited to consider what is the true character of some currently recognized virtue (*temperance* in the *Charmides*, *courage* in the *Laches*). Reflection seems to be leading us up to the conclusion that the quality under discussion is really *knowledge* of good, when we are brought to a pause by the observation that this appears to be the definition not of the particular virtue ostensibly under discussion, but of all virtue as a single whole. Formally this is treated as a proof that we are still as ignorant of the answer to the question propounded to us as we were at the outset. In fact, we are to understand, the attempt to define one virtue ends in something which is no more a definition of that virtue than of another, for the reason that in principle *all* virtue is one.

Of course, the *knowledge* with which Socrates thus identifies virtue is not anything and everything to which the name knowledge can be given; it is definitely knowledge of what is nowadays called "moral value," knowing what is my *good*. Now this leads to a real difficulty: how is such knowledge to be come by? On the one hand, if virtue is *knowledge*, the having or not having it is no matter of simple congenital endowment; men no more come into the world born good than they come into the world already born in possession of any other kind of knowledge; they have to *win* their knowledge. Yet the popularly current view that we automatically pick up "goodness," as we pick up the use of our mother-tongue, under the influence of good parents and a good social environment cannot be true. It is notorious that Pericles and the other outstanding men whom the Athenian public regards as eminently its "best men" have been quite unable to impart their own excellences to their sons; the sons have commonly been quite inferior persons. On the other hand, the eminent "sophists" profess to be able to "teach goodness," as they might teach some technical accomplishment, by a course of instruction. Now, if goodness is knowledge and nothing but knowledge, it certainly must be capable of being taught somehow; the man who has this knowledge must be able to direct another to the acquisition of it. And yet the sophistic profession of being able to teach it by a course of lectures must be hollow. The point which Socrates is represented by Plato as urging repeatedly against the sophists and their admirers is a simple one. What the sophist can teach is at best a professional speciality of some kind, how to do something which men in general cannot do. But virtue, or goodness, is no speciality with its restricted domain; its sphere is the whole domain of human conduct. And a specialism is, again, something which may be put to a good use or to an ill one, just as medical knowledge may be used to cure, but may equally be used to kill.[1] At best the sophist can impart the specialist knowledge; what he cannot impart is the "knowledge of good" which will ensure that the use made of it shall be good and not evil.

How, then, does a man learn the one kind of knowledge which it steads him most to have, knowledge of good? It is not clear that Socrates had ever reached a final solution of the problem. But we can perhaps discover the general character of the answer he would have given. According to Plato,[2] he had been struck by the

[1] It is notorious that the clever poisoner in our criminal annals is commonly a medical man.

[2] See particularly *Memo*, 81 *a*–85 *e*, where the theory is elaborately illustrated by a "lesson" in geometry given

Orphic doctrine that there are means by which the soul can be restored to remembrance of her forgotten divine origin, and from this hint he had developed the conviction that the acquisition of knowledge generally is in reality a process of "recollection" or "recognition" (*anamnesis*) in which particular sensible facts prompt or suggest the assertion of a universal principle which transcends the facts themselves. By drawing a diagram and asking a series of pertinent questions, the mathematician leads a pupil to recognize a universal proposition. He need impart no information; if the right diagram is drawn, and the

---

by Socrates to a slave-boy ignorant of the science, and *Phaedo*, 72 e ff., where there is a similar reference to the acquisition of geometrical knowledge. In both places the doctrine is brought into connection with the immortality of the soul, but it is made clear that, as a theory of what the discovery of a truth is, it is independent of this religious tenet. (It reappears, in fact, at the end of Aristotle's *Posterior Analytics*, ii, without any religious associations, as Aristotle's own account of the way in which first principles are suggested by "induction.") In the *Phaedo* (*loc. cit.*) the doctrine that "learning is just recognition" is expressly said by Simmias, speaking to Socrates, to be "the doctrine *you* are so constantly repeating." Unless we are willing to regard the *Phaedo* as a gigantic and unpardonable mystification, this seems to me proof that the theory really belongs to Socrates. For a brief statement of Plato's own allied convictions see *Ep.*, vii. 341 c, and the comments of Burnet on the passage (*Greek Philosophy*, Pt. 1, pp. 221–222).

mind of the pupil set at work on it by the right questions, it will produce the right conclusion from within, by its own action, as though from a store of truth which it already possesses unconsciously. The truth so "learned" is reached by a personal "discovery," to which the "learner" has simply been stimulated by his "teacher," and yet is also "recognized" as already implied in what the "learner" had all along known. In the same way, the acute interrogations of a Socrates who compels us to "give account" of our conduct of our lives, prompt the mind of the interrogated to "recognition" of the implications of the moral standards by which we estimate our own conduct and our neighbour's. This is the starting-point from which Plato was to develop his own theory of "philosophy" as created by the friction of minds employed in the joint pursuit after truth.

The Greek mind rightly made no distinction between the principles of private and those of public conduct, morals and "politics"; and Socrates consistently applied his conviction of the identity of "goodness" with a right estimate of "values" to the morality of the State and its statesmen. The worth of a State, and of its public men, depended, in his eyes, wholly on the degree to which the national life was based on a true scale of good. It was out of the question that, with all his practical loyalty to the constitution, he should approve of the principle of democracy, the sovereignty of the multitude who have no knowledge of the good, and have never even dreamed that such knowledge is the necessary qualification for the direction of their affairs. The judgments on the Athenian democracy of the fifth century put into his mouth in Plato's *Gorgias* and *Republic* are much harder than anything Plato has to say of democratic government on his own account in such later dialogues as the *Politicus* and the *Laws*, and it seems to me probable that the severity of these verdicts comes from Socrates rather than from Plato.[1] The very prin-

---

[1] When the language of the earlier dialogues is taken as expressing Plato's personal opinions, the more favourable judgments of the later dialogues are explained as due to the mellowing influence of time on a mind lacerated by the fate of Socrates. It may be so, but there is also always the psychological possibility that the harsher verdicts are those of Socrates himself. His disillusionment as the temper of the Athenian democracy grew narrower and harder in the course of the great war would be all the bitterer that he had grown up in the great "fifty years" before the war, and presumably had hoped and expected very different things. In a very late dialogue, the *Timaeus*, Plato makes Socrates confess to being something of a *doctrinaire* in politics, owing to his lack of personal experience of public life (*Tim.*, 19 *d*). We learn from Xenophon (*Mem.*, 1. ii 9) that sarcasms about the democratic practise of filling magistracies by sortition was one count in the case against Socrates to which he is replying.

ciple of democracy, if it can be called a principle, according to the *Republic,* is the refusal to require any superiority of intellect or character as a qualification for leadership; in the democratic community, as Nietzsche puts it, there is "one flock and no shepherd," and this is why its normal fate is to fall into the hands of an able and unscrupulous "dictator" (or, as the Greeks called him, "tyrant"). Equally severe is the condemnation pronounced by the *Gorgias* on all the famous leaders of the Athenian democracy, from Themistocles to Pericles, with the one exception, in part, of the "just" Aristides. None of them all had the knowledge of good which is the one thing needful in life, as we see from two considerations. None of them—not even Aristides—could impart any goodness he possessed to his own son, and none, except perhaps Aristides, made the public "soul" better by his tendance of it. Themistocles and Pericles and the others made Athens powerful and wealthy, but they did nothing for the *moral* of the people; they "filled the city with ships and docks, not with righteousness"; gave it worldly prosperity, but no true moral ideals. Hence we are told in the *Gorgias* that though they may have been efficient "body-servants" of the public, they have no claim to be, as true statesmen must be, its "physicians." It is clear

that Socrates really habitually used the kind of
arguments Plato ascribes to him about the in-
capacity of the Athenian public men to impart
"goodness" to their sons as a proof that their own
apparent "goodness" was not the genuine thing.
In the *Meno* Anytus is introduced expressly to
warn him that this depreciation of the national
heroes is a dangerous sport—a plain indication of
Plato's belief that it had much to do with pro-
voking the attack which ended in his prosecution.

From the Socratic point of view, the proper
organization of society would be one in which
every man's social status and function, as statesman, soldier, or producer, is determined by the
nature of the work his aptitudes, understanding,
and character fit him to discharge. This is precisely the ideal which is embodied in outline in
the account of the ideal city which fills the earlier
books of Plato's *Republic*. So far, the scheme may
truly be said to be directly of Socratic inspiration.
How far any of its details are actually of Socratic
origin is another question, though it is suggestive
that this seems to be so with one of its most
original features, the proposal to admit women
on the same terms as men to public employment, military and civil, and the education which
qualifies for it. That Socrates actually entertained

an ideal of this kind seems to be shown by the fact that Aeschines also in his dialogue *Aspasia* dwelt on the political capacity of Aspasia herself and others, and the military ability believed to have been shown by the real or legendary Persian princess Rhodogyne. Xenophon also incidentally puts into the mouth of his Socrates the thesis that, with the necessary training, a woman is capable of the same things as a man.[1]

2. *Theory of Knowledge and Scientific Method.*—Aristotle remarks in the *Metaphysics* that "two things must in justice be ascribed to Socrates, inductive arguments and universal definition."[2] This does not take us very far; Aristotle

---

[1] See the fragments of the *Aspasia* in the editions of Krauss and Dittmar. Xenophon's testimony to Socrates' belief that "a woman is no worse endowed by nature than a man, though not his equal in judgment or physical strength," will be found at *Symp.*, ii. 9. For evidence from Xenophon to the demand of *knowledge* as the one qualification for sovereignty, see *Mem.*, III. ix. 10, and compare the whole of III. vi. where Socrates dissuades Glaucon from a premature entrance on public life by exposing his ignorance of military and financial statistics. That Xenophon speaks only of such ignorance of facts, not of the graver ignorance of "moral values," strikes me as characteristic of the man.

[2] *Met. M.,* 1078 *b* 27. Some good recent German students make a point of denying that Socrates was really interested in "definition." This is true in the sense that his concern was not with theoretical labels for their own sake, but with a practical rule of conduct. What justi-

is clearly intending less to give us a complete characterization of Socrates than to specify certain constituents of his own philosophy as derived from him, and he seems to be basing his statement simply on his reading of Plato's dialogues, which illustrate the point abundantly. Xenophon's apologetic interest in the soundness of his old teacher's moral lessons leaves him little inclination to talk about anything else. Our chances of being able to discover something more about Socrates as a thinker on other than strictly ethical topics stand or fall with the historical truth of the autobiographical narrative put into his mouth in Plato's *Phaedo*.[1] Now it seems to me, as I have already said, that we are bound to take this narrative as being substantially what Plato regarded as historical fact. The alternative is to suppose that an account of what Socrates said of himself on the last day of his life, in the presence of a number of intimate friends who were all living when that account was published, and certain to read it, is a fiction which all these readers would immediately detect. No one is really courageous

fies Aristotle's way of expressing himself is that he is thinking of the formal structure of such works as *Charmides*, *Laches*, *Protagoras*, *Meno*, *Republic* iv.

[1] *Phaedo*, 96 *a*–100 *c*. The whole passage should be studied carefully with the annotations to it in Burnet's edition of the dialogue (Oxford, 1911).

enough to be thorough with such a theory. Everybody, for instance, accepts as fact the story of the introduction of Socrates to the book of Anaxagoras, and his disappointment with it, though we have no evidence for the fact beyond the statement of the *Phaedo*. But that statement in the *Phaedo* is merely the beginning of a coherent narrative, and it is therefore incumbent on us in consistency either to accept the rest of the narrative as substantially accurate, or to treat the initial statement with the same scepticism as all that follows it. I have little doubt for myself which is the more reasonable course. No sane man, of course, would deny that Plato, like every great artist, mixed his own mind with his object. It is quite another matter to assert that he consciously presents us with his own features in a pretended portrait of Socrates.[1]

According to the *Phaedo*, then, the immediate effect on Socrates of his discovery that Anaxagoras dogmatized about Nature in the same arbitrary fashion as his precursors was to lead him to strike out a new *method* in the search for truth. If we cannot discover the truth about

---

[1] A great portrait-painter always puts his own personality into his portraits. If he were an inferior artist, the portrait would be different. But he does not give his sitters his own nose or eyebrows.

things by direct inspection of the things themselves, we may attempt to reach it by examining the *statements*, or *theories* (*logoi*), which we make about them. The apparent indirectness of the procedure is Socrates' reason for humorously proceeding to depreciate it as the "make-shift of an amateur." Really, of course, he holds that it affords us our one and only chance of getting any genuine knowledge. The procedure he is describing is precisely that which, as we see from Xenophon,[1] as well as from Plato, he called *dialectic*, a name which properly means the method of "conversation." The thought which explains the use of the name is that truth has to be reached by dint of dialogue, or debate, which may be carried on between two inquirers, or also within the heart of a single inquirer, as his "soul" questions itself and answers its own questions. The truth, which is not to be discovered by any direct inspection of "facts," may be beaten out in the critical confrontation of rival interpretations of them. It comes, when it comes, as the conclusion to a debate.

[1] A chapter of some length in the *Memorabilia* (IV. vi.) is devoted to illustrations of the way in which Socrates made those who associated with him "more dialectical." He did this, according to Xenophon, by urging them to think precisely and to express their thought intelligibly.

It is this method of confrontation of rival "arguments" or "theories" which Aristophanes wittily and wickedly burlesques in the *Clouds*. Protagoras also had said, in a very different sense, that "there are two arguments about everything," two sides to every case, and that the art of effective advocacy which he taught aims at making the "weaker case"—that which unskilfully presented would have got the worse with the audience—the "stronger." Aristophanes puts on this harmless dictum the sense that the object of advocacy is to make the morally worse case appear the better, and then transfers the procedure to Socrates, with the result that the rival "arguments" are brought on the stage as Virtue and Vice, and Vice, of course, drives Virtue out of the field. This is pure burlesque, but it presupposes as its foundation the fact that, in the infancy of Plato, Socrates was already known as specially interested in the confrontation of "arguments" of some kind.

The *Phaedo* gives us a fairly full account of the nature of the procedure. The method is that Socrates starts from some proposition which, on any grounds, commends itself to him as presumably true. This he calls his initial *hypothesis*, and he proceeds to ask himself "what must follow if this is admitted," that is, to deduce its consequences. The truth of the initial *hypothesis* being at present unquestioned, whatever follows from it is also set down as true, and whatever conflicts with it as false. Thus the assumption of the method is simply that truth is a coherent system, and that nothing which conflicts with a true principle can be true. We must note, of course, that the assumed principle which Socrates calls his *hypothesis* is not taken to be hypothetical in the sense of being a "pure supposal." Socrates takes it as the starting-point of an argument because he presumes it to be true, or because it is common ground to himself and the other party to the discussion. On the other hand, there is no question of asserting it as a self-evident and final truth. It may be called in question, and in that case requires to be defended by being deduced as a consequence from some more ultimate and less disputable *hypothesis*. The important rule of method is that the question what consequences follow from the *hypothesis*, and the question whether the *hypothesis* itself is true, must be kept distinct. So long as we are still concerned with the former question, that of the consequences, the *hypothesis* itself must be left unquestioned.

So far, the method ascribed to Socrates in the *Phaedo* is clearly in principle that which has

7

proved itself the one path to truth in scientific theory down to our own time. The contrast drawn between the direct procedure of the Ionian physicists, which had led nowhere, and the method of studying things in the "statements" we make about them is precisely that also drawn by De Morgan between the erroneous method of Bacon, who assumes that facts are there to *draw a theory from*, and the sound method of Newton, who treats the facts as there *to test theory by*.[1] The one notable difference is that Socrates makes no special reference to the *verification* of theory by the confrontation of theoretical consequences with observational fact. Verification, however, finds its proper place in the elaboration of the Socratic thought by Plato and his Academy, whose technical name for a scientific theory which clearly accounts for all the relevant observed facts was an *hypothesis* which "saves appearances." (The "appearances" are the facts as observed; to "save" them is to account for them all in a coherent way.) Of course, neither Socrates nor Plato could have contemplated the modern extension of verification by experiments devised expressly for the purpose.

So far there is some independent evidence that

[1] A. De Morgan, *A Budget of Paradoxes* (ed. 2), i. 88.

the statements of the *Phaedo* about the method of Socrates are historical. Xenophon was aware that his practice, when one of his theses was disputed, was to "bring the whole discussion back to the *hypothesis*," that is, the initial position which was common ground to himself and his opponent,[1] though this, of course, may only mean that Xenophon had read the *Phaedo* and seen no reason to distrust its statements. It is more significant to my mind that Plato himself apparently makes Protagoras refer, without any further explanation, to the method of taking some proposition as an *hypothesis* which is not to be questioned so long as we are concerned with discovering its consequences, as something distinctively characteristic of Socrates, in a dialogue feigned to have been held before Plato's own birth.[2] We can see, moreover, from what quarter Socrates is likely to have derived the suggestion of the method. Rigorous deduction of the consequences of an *hypothesis* was the peculiar method of the famous Zeno of Elea, though it was the *hypotheses* of his opponents which he treated in this way, and his object was to discredit them

[1] *Mem.*, IV. vi. 13.

[2] *Prot.*, 351 *e*. The name *hypothesis* is not used here, but Protagoras proposes to Socrates to discuss the thesis that the good is pleasure "in your regular way," by working out its consequences.

by showing that they led to impossible consequences, as he is made to explain himself to the
youthful Socrates in Plato's *Parmenides*.[1]

As far as this many, if not most, careful students of the evidence would probably be willing
to follow us. Most of them may decline to take
the further step of accepting as fundamentally
true to fact what the narrative of the *Phaedo*
goes on to say about the nature of the particular
hypothesis adopted by Socrates himself as the
basis of his thinking. This, it is said, is nothing
but the famous "Theory of Ideas," and it is commonly assumed without proof, or with no proof
but a few ambiguous expressions in Aristotle, that
this doctrine was discovered by Plato for the
first time after the death of Socrates. For my own
part, I feel with Burnet that it is inconceivable
that any thinker should introduce an eminently
original discovery of his own to the world by
representing it as something which had long been
familiar to a number of living contemporaries
who were certain to read his work and detect any
misrepresentation. I hold, therefore, that we must
accept the statements of the *Phaedo* as substantially true to fact, and have to explain the evidence of Aristotle, if we accept it at all for more
than his own private conjecture, in a way which

[1] *Parm.*, 128 *c–e*.

will not conflict with Plato. We must remember, of course, that Plato has mixed his own personality with his object in the very act of depicting it, but we must take this to be done inevitably and without conscious distortion of truth.

The problem which had perplexed Socrates was that of the "cause of coming-to-be and ceasing-to-be." Why does a thing make its appearance in the world or disappear from it? Why does a thing come to exhibit a quality which it had not before, or to lose one which it had? The physicists had their answer to this question; they found the causes of these changes in physical agents, which they assigned variously and arbitrarily. Reflection on the implications of the thesis of Anaxagoras about *Mind* as the source of the order in the world suggested to Socrates that these physical agents, whatever they may be, are at best only *concomitant* causes, or indispensable conditions, of an event; the real cause is, in every case, that it is *best* that things should be as they are, and in a mind-ordered world everything will be disposed as it is *best* that it should be. In this way, Socrates introduced into philosophy that "teleological" or "finalist" conception of the order of the universe as realizing an end of absolute value which was to be fully worked out and transmitted to later times as the chief heritage of Greek philosophical thought by Plato, Aristotle, and Plotinus.

The abandonment of the old *naïf* method of trying to discover truth by a simple inspection of "facts" meant, of course, that Socrates could not dream of learning by direct inspection what the particular details of the world-order are, and why it is *best* that they should be as they are. But his conviction that there is an intelligible order in everything, and that it is a wise order, gave him a characteristic point of view from which to approach the question why a thing comes to be or ceases to be, acquires or loses a character. He speaks of this attitude in the *Phaedo* as nothing novel to his auditors, but one of which they have repeatedly heard from him. If a thing becomes what it was not before, if, for example, it becomes beautiful, this is always for one and the same reason, that Beauty has "become present to" the thing; if it ceases to be beautiful, Beauty has "withdrawn" from it. Or, in an alternative phrase, a thing which is beautiful is so just because, and so long as, it "partakes" of Beauty; a figure is triangular just so long as, and because it "partakes of" *the* triangle; and so forth. Beauty, or, as the Greek language expresses it, "*the* Beautiful," "*the* triangle," and the like, are what in this doctrine are called Forms or Patterns (*eidē*,

ideai),[1] and a thing is what it is, has the characters
it has, because it "partakes" of the Forms of
which it does "partake." And there are the following important points to be noted about these
Forms. (1) The "things which partake of a Form"
are all perishable; they begin to be and cease to
be, but the Form, Beauty, *the* Triangle, etc.,
neither begins to be, nor ceases to be; it is strictly
what Dr. Whitehead calls an "*eternal* object."
(2) The things which we perceive by our senses
only "partake of," or "resemble," the Forms imperfectly. We never see a stick which is flawlessly
straight, or a patch which is exactly and perfectly
triangular, and we never perhaps meet with an act
of perfect justice; we only see approximately
straight sticks and approximately triangular
patches, and come across acts of approximate
justice. But "the straight line" or "the triangle"
about which the geometer tells us is perfectly
straight or triangular, and the justice of which the
moralist talks as a duty is perfect justice. (3) The
things which "partake of the Form" may be indefinitely many; the Form itself is strictly one.
Even in geometry, where we talk of many tri-

---

[1] But it is misleading to call them, as they have so long
been called, *Ideas*. That suggests to us that they are some
one's *thoughts*, "ideas in some one's head," precisely
what the theory does *not* mean.

angles which are all assumed to be perfectly triangular, what the geometer is interested in proving is not the properties of this triangle or that
triangle, but those of "the" triangle.[1] And it is
always the Form, never this or that thing which
"partakes of" a Form, which is the object of
which we are talking in science. I *know* as a
scientific truth that any two sides of the triangle
must be greater together than the third side; I do
not *know* that two sides of this patch before me
must be greater than the third, since I do not
know that this visible patch really is triangular.

We should like, of course, if we could, to know
something more of these Forms. Of what things
are there Forms (and, consequently, of what
things can we have scientific knowledge)? And,
again, do the Forms constitute a system of any
kind? We can see from the polemical allusions of
Aristotle that at a later date Plato's Academy
had answers, not always concordant answers, to
these questions, and that Aristotle found all these
answers unsatisfactory. But we are not entitled
to read back into the *Phaedo* developments which
belong to Plato's old age, and we may even doubt
whether in the *Republic* Plato may not be uncon-

[1]We see this in an interesting way from the language,
e.g., of Analytical Geometry about "*the* equation to the
circle," or of Arithmetic about "*the* number six."

sciously "colouring" his picture of Socrates more than he knows as his argument advances. From the examples given in the *Phaedo* itself it would seem that what Socrates was chiefly thinking of is, on the one side, the objects of which the mathematician can give us perfect and absolute definitions in geometry and arithmetic, and on the other the ideal standards and norms of the moralist (*the* number 3, *the* triangle, *the* Just, and the like). And this impression is borne out for us by a dialogue written by Plato at a late period in his career, the *Parmenides,* in which Socrates is expounding his theory to the great Eleatic philosophers Parmenides and Zeno, and defending it, not very satisfactorily, against their criticism. He is made there to say[1] that he feels quite sure that there are Forms of such things as Like and Unlike, Unity, Multitude, Just, Good, but very doubtful whether there are Forms of Man, Fire, Water, and still more doubtful about Hair, Mud, Dirt. In fact, he is sure of his ground in Mathematics and Morals, but very unsure of it everywhere else. We may infer that the first impulse to the formation of the theory came from reflection on mathematical and moral truth. This is what we should expect if the doctrine originated with Socrates, and if Socrates were the man Plato depicts. The

[1]*Parm.,* 129–130.

very terminology used seems to come in the first instance from Pythagorean mathematics. There is clear evidence that the word *eidos* was the old Pythagorean name for "figure," a sense of the word which persists in some stereotyped phrases in Euclid and other third-century geometers, though their common word for *figure* is a different one (*schema*).[1] And Plato frequently represents Socrates as deeply impressed by the need for moral standards by which controversies about right and wrong may be determined, as disputes about area or volume are settled by an appeal to geometry, or disagreements about weight by resort to the balance.

We see that the doctrine is a first attempt to do justice to the *a priori* factor in knowledge, the *universality* and *necessity* of scientific truths most conspicuously evident in the propositions of pure mathematics and pure ethics, and that those disciplines are taken as the model of what all science should be. We understand thus why the Forms have been identified by later philosophers with "universals," "concepts," "class-notions." But to speak of them so involves a really unhistorical transposition of a simpler thought. It is

[1] The same sense of "patterns" accounts for our language about figures of speech, and figures of the syllogism.

to make Socrates talk like Aristotle, or Kant, and this cannot be done without risk of misunderstanding, though his doctrine is the ultimate source of theirs. If we would avoid all such misunderstandings, it is best to say simply that the Form is that—whatever it may be—which we mean to denote whenever we use a significant "common name" as the subject of a strictly and absolutely true proposition, the object about which such a proposition makes a true assertion. Such objects, not the sensible things disclosed in bodily perception, are, according to Socrates, the most real things there are, and the only things which are fully real. The soul, as we saw, has one single fundamental activity, that of *knowing* realities as they really are, and it is only in knowing the Forms that this activity is successfully discharged. Where the mind is not face to face with a Form, we have only *opinion* or *belief*, a *belief* which may, of course, in many cases be quite sufficient for the needs of everyday life, but we have not *knowledge;* the element of "*necessary* connection" is missing.

Do the Forms, which are the proper objects of genuine knowledge, form an organized whole or system? They should do so, no doubt, since, according to the *Phaedo*, the whole doctrine of them as the explanation of "coming-into-being and ceasing-to-be" is inspired by the still more ultimate conviction that in a mind-permeated world all things are ordered as it is best they should be, and the Good—itself a Form—is therefore the cause of the whole order. This is strictly in accord with a famous passage of the *Republic*,[1] where Socrates speaks of the Good, or Form of good, as holding the same supreme and central position in the realm of Forms apprehended by the intellect which its "offspring" the Sun holds in the visible world. As the sun in the visible world is the source at once of the life of the things we see and the light by which they are seen, so the good in the world disclosed to thought is the source at once of the reality of the Forms we apprehend and of the knowledge by which they are apprehended. And as the sun, though the source of light and growth, is not the same thing as either, so the good is neither "being" nor "knowledge," but something which is the transcendent source of both. But Socrates is made to confess that as it is the supreme feat of corporeal vision to be able to look on the sun, so it is the supreme and most difficult achievement of the mind to know the Good. He himself, in this passage, confesses his own inability to speak of it in any language but that of parable and metaphor. Plato has

[1] *Rep.*, 506 *d*–509 *b*.

been commonly thought in this passage to be talking of a personal speculation of his own of which the Master whose voice he is borrowing had never dreamed. In view of the intimate connection made in the "autobiographical" pages of the *Phaedo* between the *hypothesis* of Forms and the conviction that the Good is the universal cause, I find it difficult to subscribe to this opinion. I should rather judge that the language and imagery of this splendid passage are those of Plato in his "golden prime," but the thought is one directly necessitated by the meditations born of the first falling-in with the book of Anaxagoras.

It is clear that the doctrine of Forms, in the shape in which, as I hold, we must be prepared to ascribe it to Socrates, creates difficulties as well as removes them. In particular, it leaves wholly unexplained the relation of the Form to sensible fact which it calls its "presence," or its being "participated in." Is what we call a sensible thing merely a temporary assemblage of Forms, or "universals," and if it is more, what else is it? No one has pointed out these difficulties more incisively than Plato himself in his dialogue *Parmenides*, and it seems at least plain that the final form of Plato's own teaching, which we have to reconstruct imperfectly from the puzzling hints of Aristotle, was an attempt to find an answer to the problem.

Aristotle himself was so perplexed by the results that he comes to treat the whole doctrine of Forms itself as a mistaken attempt to separate the "universal characters" of individual sensible things from the things themselves, and then to set up these "abstractions" as a second set of super-sensible things which somehow produce the things we see and handle. It is, he says, as though a man who had to count a number of articles were to fancy that he must begin by doubling it. He believed himself to have got rid once for all of an unreal and insoluble problem by his own formula that the "form" only exists *in* the individual sensible thing, and is just its "essential character." Yet the problem is still with us, in spite of Aristotle, as a very real *crux* in the latest attempts to furnish a philosophy of the sciences. We still find ourselves asking what is the "status" of "scientific objects." Just what *are* the things of which the mathematician and the physicist discourse? Or again, what is a moral "ideal"? And what is the relation of the "scientific object" to the things we touch or see, and how, again, are "value" and "fact" related? Natural and moral philosophy are still far from having answered these questions with finality, and even further from having escaped the necessity of asking them. The unique greatness of Socrates lies in the fact that he was the first man in the world to raise them with the clear understanding of what he was doing.

Several of the companions of Socrates were active after his death as heads of philosophical schools, and one, Antisthenes, was a voluminous writer. It has been common to speak of these men and their followers as "minor Socratics." It is, to my mind, very doubtful how far this language, which reflects the artificial schematism of Alexandrian biography, is justified. The Megarian opponents of Aristotle in the fourth century, their contemporaries, Diogenes and the other eccentrics popularly nicknamed Cynics, the Hedonist moralists of Cyrene in the third, were affiliated to Socrates through Euclides, Antisthenes, and Aristippus respectively. But there is no evidence of the existence of any Cyrenaic school before the days of the successors of Alexander; the Megarics, who showed themselves pugnacious opponents of Aristotle, clearly held views not to be reconciled with the strict Monism ascribed by all our authorities to Euclides; though Diogenes and his imitators professed a great reverence for Antisthenes, it is not clear that they regarded themselves as in any way related to him as a "founder." And Euclides, Aristippus, Antisthenes, were all rather admiring friends than "disciples" of Socrates. The doctrines of Euclides were a direct inheritance from the Eleatics; Aristippus is expressly recorded to have had no doctrines at all; the paradoxical views for which Antisthenes is chiefly remembered, his denial of the possibility of contradiction, and the like, come not from Socrates, but from the "sophists." For all purposes of importance, Socrates had just one "successor" —Plato.

BIBLIOGRAPHICAL NOTE

It would be impossible to furnish a work like the present with a complete conspectus of the enormous mass of literature—good and bad—connected with the subject of Socrates and his significance. I must content myself with mentioning a very few recent works which, in my opinion, an English reader will find useful or stimulating.

BURNET, J. *Greek Philosophy, Part One, Thales to Plato.* (Oxford, 1914.)

BURNET, J. *The Socratic Doctrine of the Soul,* in *Proceedings of the British Academy* for 1915–1916, pp. 235 ff.

BURNET, J. Article "Socrates," in Hastings' *Encyclopaedia of Religion and Ethics,* vol. xi.

BURNET, J. The *Phaedo* of Plato. (Oxford, 1911.)

BURNET, J. The *Euthyphro, Apology* and *Crito* of Plato. (Oxford, 1924.)

TAYLOR, A. E. *Plato's Biography of Socrates*, in *Proceedings of the British Academy* for 1917–1918, pp. 93 ff.

ROBIN, L. Editions of the *Phaedo* and *Symposium* of Plato, in the *Collection des Universités de France*.

RITTER, C. *Sokrates*. Tübingen, 1931.

BRUNS, I. *Das literarische Porträt der Griechen* (1896).

ADAM, J. Editions of the *Apology* (1905), *Crito* (1891), *Euthyphro* (1890), and *Protagoras* (1893) of Plato. (Cambridge University Press.)

For the historical background of the life of Socrates I would refer the reader acquainted with German primarily to vols. iv and v of E. Meyer's *Geschichte des Altertums*, though the older narrative by Grote still retains most of its value.

I have made little reference to the nineteenth-century literature, as I hold that, with all its merits, most of it pursued a false line in distrusting the narrative of Plato. But I would specially commend for its scholarship and sanity out of this vast literature the work of Grote, *Plato and the other Companions of Socrates*. The Alexandrian version of the life of Socrates is most readily accessible to the English reader in the text and translation of Diogenes Laertius by R. D. Hicks (Loeb Classical Library, Heinemann, 1925), where it occupies pp. 148–177 of vol. i. It may be worth while to mention two sane and instructive works dealing with the "erotic" side of Socrates as depicted by Plato: R. Lagerborg, *Die platonische Liebe*, Leipzig, 1926, and the briefer essay of C. Ritter, *Platonische Liebe*, Tübingen, 1931. I would particularly commend the former and larger book.

Much that is of value will be found in the large works of C. Ritter and U. von Wilamowitz-Moellendorff, both entitled *Platon*, but Socrates is, of course, only incidentally the subject of these. A good conspectus of recent theories about the worth of the various authorities will be found in A. Diès, *Autour de Platon*, Paris, 1927, vol. i. pp. 127–243.

INDEX

ANCHOR BOOKS

DOLPHIN BOOKS AND DOLPHIN MASTERS

The bold face M indicates a Dolphin Master. Dolphin Masters are Dolphin Books in the editions of greatest importance to the teacher and student. In selecting the Dolphin Masters, the editors have taken particular pains to choose copies of the most significant edition (usually the first) by obtaining original books or their facsimiles or by having reproductions made of library copies of particularly rare editions. Facsimiles of original title pages and other appropriate material from the first edition are included in many Masters.

FICTION

POETRY AND DRAMA

HISTORY AND BIOGRAPHY

PHILOSOPHY AND RELIGION